ADUs
THE PERFECT HOUSING SOLUTION

SHERI KOONES

Gibbs Smith

For my dear husband, Rob

First Edition
28 27 26 25 24   5 4 3 2 1

Text © 2024 Sheri Koones
Front cover photo: © 2024 Alyssa Lee Photography
Back cover photos:
    Top left © 2024 Alyssa Lee Photography
    Top middle © 2024 Zachary Cornwell
    Top right © 2024 Erik Meadows
    Middle left © 2024 Emi Kitawaki
    Middle center © 2024 Andrea Calo
    Middle right © 2024 Art Gray
    Bottom left © 2024 Jamie Wolf
    Author photo © 2024 Allen Green

Photographic credits are additionally found on the opening
page of each chapter.

Published by
Gibbs Smith
P.O. Box 667
Layton, Utah 84041
1.800.835.4993 orders
www.gibbs-smith.com

Designed by Virginia Snow

Printed and bound in China
Gibbs Smith books are printed on paper produced from
sustainable PEFC-certified forest/controlled wood source.
Learn more at www.pefc.org.

Library of Congress Control Number: 2023945637
ISBN: 978-1-4236-6525-0

CONTENTS

INTRODUCTION

Since the early 2000s, I've been writing about residential construction, with a growing concern for energy efficiency, sustainability, and small-sized constructions. In my book *Prefabulous Small Houses*, written in 2016, I profiled my first Accessory Dwelling Unit (ADU) located in Vancouver, Canada, and was taken with the practicality of this new type (to me) of construction. I began to see this trend growing and its importance in the future of residential housing. With the huge shortage of housing and the abundance of downsizing boomers and millennials looking for housing, ADUs are clearly one of the best solutions.

I have since included ADUs in all my subsequent books and have seen an upward growth in this type of construction ever since. In the many presentations I give in libraries and conferences, the majority of questions are always about ADUs. With this growing interest, I was motivated to explore this trend and all the possibilities in types of construction, locations, designs, and so on.

ADUs are one of the fastest growing trends in residential housing in North America. Every month it seems another municipality is attempting to pass zoning regulations to allow ADUs in their areas or is updating those already in place. The growth of ADUs has been spurred on by the decline in entry-level housing options, the desire for easier access to jobs, and the increase in multigenerational living (with older and younger adults wanting to live close to family). ADUs are becoming increasingly popular as new legislation is adopted to allow ADUs in more municipalities and as more companies are either specializing in ADU design and construction or are adding ADUs to their regular design and construction offerings.

Because this is such a growing trend, I wanted to research the many options available in style, locations, building types, and formats for ADUs. In researching this book, I looked at hundreds of ADUs and selected the ones that would best demonstrate the many options available. I have included examples of homes all over North America—urban to suburban to rural and built in all types of climates. In this book you will find some of the most beautiful, efficient, and well-designed ADUs in North America, plus sidebars to define some of the material and system options to build these units. There is also a resource list where those considering building an ADU can find the architects, builders, manufacturers, and materials to make their journey easier.

There are still a lot of questions about this very recent technology, and in this next section, I'll answer many of the queries I get from consumers interested in ADUs.

WHAT IS AN ADU?

An ADU is a secondary home on the property of a main house that has its own entrance and contains, minimally, a bathroom, a kitchen or kitchenette, and a sleeping area. It can be a separate unit, or it can be built in place of an existing garage, built over a garage, or attached to the primary home as an addition or basement apartment. An ADU is referred to by several names—granny-flat, detached accessory dwelling unit (DADU), in-law suite, casita, laneway house, and more. There is also a Junior ADU or JADU, which is located within the floor area of an original single-family house. An ADU is considered part of the main residence, and, in most cases, it must be sold with that residence, although some municipalities are trying to change that regulation. As of this writing, there are currently about 1.5 million ADUs in the United States and that number is growing at a rate of about 9 percent per year.

THE COST OF AN ADU

It is difficult to cite a universal price for an ADU because of the many factors that go into this calculation. The cost of building an ADU is dependent on its location, size, configuration, cost of materials, cost of permits, local labor costs, and the complexity of the unit. Other factors include whether it is part of the main house, a conversion from a garage, or a new detached structure. The size of the ADU will be dependent on local zoning laws as well as personal preference. On average ADUs are between 600 and 1,200 square feet, but there are exceptions to these figures, both larger and smaller (as demonstrated in this book). The most positive financial factor in building an ADU is that the land is free, which is often one of the costliest parts of any construction.

MOTIVATIONS TO BUILD AN ADU

A big motivation to build an ADU is the vast shortage of housing, particularly affordable housing, in many areas of North America. An ADU provides housing within a community that blends in with the neighborhood, in contrast to large multiplexes and apartment houses which alter the nature of an area. An ADU is generally hidden within or behind the house, minimally changing the nature of the community.

Some homeowners are motivated to build an ADU because it can increase the value of their home by as much as 35 percent in those areas where they are zoned.

Another major motivating factor is the growing aging population that is more active and vital than previous generations. An ADU can help finance retirement for many homeowners. They can either rent it on their property, move into the ADU themselves and rent out their main house, or live in a multigenerational environment with family.

An ADU provides housing for those people looking for a smaller house. Millennials in general have smaller families, so they need less space, and, being an environmentally conscious generation, they prefer to use less energy to heat and cool their homes. Boomers need less space when they are empty-nesters, and many try to reduce their expenses when they stop working. Both groups are looking for less residential maintenance, preferring to spend their free time with family and recreational activities. An ADU is the perfect solution for these groups and others as well.

An ADU is often in an area where other housing is too costly, and it offers an opportunity to live in a location that would otherwise not be available. It provides housing for the local workforce, offering them an affordable place to live in the areas where they work. This includes seasonal workers in beach and ski resort areas. It also provides an opportunity to live closer to jobs and cut down on commuting time. An ADU often provides housing that is close to transportation, schools, shopping, and entertainment.

ADUs can also provide additional income to help pay for the homeowners' main house and often help with their retirement expenses.

HISTORY OF ADUS

ADUs were initially spurred on in Canada by the shortage of housing and an economic crisis following World War II, where one of the earlier methods of building ADUs was in the laneways where garages once stood. ADUs are a more recent development in the United States, with more and more cities and municipalities permitting them over the last several years. The growth of ADUs in the United States is mainly due to the decline in the number of affordable homes and relaxed restrictions on the size and scope of these units.

ADU CONFIGURATIONS OR FORMATS

Some ADUs are built where a garage or carport once stood, and some are built atop a garage or even in a converted Tuff Shed Garage. Several of the ADUs in this book are connected to the main house. One is connected to the main house with an elevated walkway. Several of the units are free standing. Other ADUs are located in the main house's basement or loft.

MULTIGENERATIONAL LIVING

An ADU offers an opportunity for multigenerational living for older adults who no longer need large homes and would like to live near their children, while still maintaining the independence and privacy of each family group. When multiple generations live close to each other, they can share resources and give families an opportunity to spend more time with each other—parents can help with childcare and adult children can help elderly parents who might need extra assistance.

Several of the ADUs mentioned are built with Universal Design (UD) features for aging-in-place for themselves or for their parents. One has an elevator so parents can live there in the future. Another built their ADU to currently generate extra income for themselves, but with several UD features to potentially create housing for their aging parents, and eventually provide themselves with a comfortable place to age in place. Several of the houses contain curbless showers as a safety measure for themselves, their parents, and visitors.

There are situations where adult children live in the ADU and when their families become larger, they swap homes with their empty-nester parents in the main house. Some homeowners prefer to live in the smaller space the ADU affords and gift or sell the main house to an adult child.

AN AFFORDABLE HOME IN THE COMMUNITY

Many young people find they are priced out of living in the neighborhood where they grew up. An ADU allows them to live in that neighborhood at a more affordable cost. Living on the homestead property in an ADU provides a less expensive living situation for an adult child, while maintaining their privacy. Even without family members living close by, some people are attracted to certain neighborhoods and an ADU offers them a reasonably priced option.

PROVIDING NEEDED ADDITIONAL SPACE

Some homeowners like where they are living but need additional space for a variety of reasons, such as working from home, exercising, entertaining, and so on. Building an ADU can provide the needed extra space without having to move away from a house that holds fond memories and that they already enjoy. With so many people working from home, whether full or part-time, an ADU offers the essence of a comfortable, quiet workspace. An ADU also is frequently used as supplemental housing for short- or long-term stays, where family and friends can stay and have privacy.

BOOSTING FINANCES AND PROVIDING NEEDED RENTALS

Some people also buy or build a house with the intention of adding an ADU to help finance their main home. The ADU may be used for short- or long-term rentals and provide needed income.

An ADU can be part of a homeowner's retirement plan. Some homeowners initially live in the main house and rent out the ADU while they are working. When they retire, they might move into the ADU and rent out their main house, which frequently offsets the cost of building the new unit. When it is not rented, it can provide additional space for family and friends.

Often homeowners are ready to downsize to a smaller space when their children move out of the house. An ADU provides an opportunity for them to remain in the area by moving into the smaller space and renting out the main house. Carefully designed with aging-in-place in mind, the ADU should have fewer steps and less upkeep. In other cases, the ADU may provide a place for a caretaker to live.

RESTRICTIONS BY AREA

Municipalities have their own regulations regarding ADUs: how many may be on the property, how big they can be, who can live in them, what style they may be, how many parking spaces are required on the property, and so on. ADUs must meet the local zoning laws—some more stringent than others.

In some areas the owner of the property or a family member must live in either the main house or the ADU. In other areas, such as Atlanta, Georgia, the owners do not have to live in either unit. Count on there being restrictions as to the size of the ADU, the setbacks, the height, the design, and so on in your area. As this book is going to print, there are many locations where local governments are still negotiating what regulations they will put in place for future units. Some areas still have not allowed ADUs at all. If you live in a Homeowner's Association, be aware that they will also have their own restrictions and regulations, in addition to the local governments. Before anyone considers building an ADU they must first check with the local municipality to make sure they can be built in the area and what the regulations are. Here are some additional questions people should ask:

- How big can the ADU be?

- Can more than one ADU be built on the property?

- How large do the setbacks have to be? What are the height and size restrictions?

- Is there a particular design the ADU must adhere to?

- Do owners have to occupy one of the units? Can one or both the main house and ADU be rented?

- Do the main residence and ADU need to have separate utilities, or can they share utilities?

- Is it necessary to provide a parking space for the ADU?

- Are there additional restrictions?

ONE-STOP SHOPS

Some companies provide predesigned ADUs, where the new owner can just tweak a design to meet their personal needs. These companies may provide construction as well as design services. This can be an advantage to the homeowner since these "one-stop" companies will provide multiple services for the homeowner—surveyors, civil engineers, structural engineers, architects, permitting experts, contractors, and so on. This saves time in the permitting process, less time for bidding, and negotiation with one company, rather than several. They already have most of the pricing data available, and they can go to contract quicker. Construction also moves more quickly since their builders, in many cases, have built these units multiple times.

MUNICIPAL INCENTIVES

Recently several municipalities have been providing incentives to homeowners to build an ADU in exchange for the homeowner renting it to lower-income people and homeless families. Some of these programs involve deferred equity loans, permitting fee waivers, free project management, affordable design, monetary subsidies, favorable loans, and so on. None of these types of ADUs were available to include here at this time. To find out about these incentives, check the websites providing information in your area such as https://villahomes.com and https://hcr.ny.gov/plus-one-adu-program, and several others.

HOW ADUS ARE BUILT

ADUs can be built on-site, or they can be built with a variety of prefabricated methods. Many of the ADUs in this book are stick built. Other ADUs are built using prefabricated construction. Examples in this book include a kit ADU and several panelized ADUs. And there were several built with structural insulated panels (SIPs).

All the ADUs in this book were built with energy and green features considered in the construction, particularly in California with its strict energy laws. They were built in different configurations, in different styles, and for a variety of reasons, but all were built with great creativity and modern technology. I hope this book will provide inspiration for those considering building an ADU, help for those ready to begin the process, and information for those just dreaming of building them for the future.

DRAWBACKS TO ADUS

In some areas people find the approval and permitting process difficult when they set out to build an ADU. In other areas people complain the fees are excessive. There can also be design constraints that make it difficult for homeowners to build the unit they would optimally prefer.

Currently many municipalities are restricting ADUs in their areas. This can be due to the fear of added traffic in the area and the possibility of changing the nature of the neighborhood. There have also been cases of ADUs being built at heights that limit the view of neighboring houses. This may require stricter regulations in those areas where these problems are occurring. In general, however, most of the ADUs are built behind the main houses and are out of view of neighboring houses. In addition, many of those homeowners I interviewed for this book tried to build units that fit in with the local neighborhood design.

There are still issues with ADUs that need to be worked out, and they aren't the perfect answer for everyone. However, the positives of building an ADU really outweigh any negatives that may arise. ADUs are adding density to communities without homeowners having to build larger homes and optimally without large multiplexes being built for additional housing in the area. Building standards for them are often stricter than for the main house, making them environmentally friendly. They provide housing for people who might not be able to otherwise live in these communities, while adding needed income for homeowners. These units allow some people to age in place, which might not be possible without the added income from the ADU, or the extra space for a caregiver or family member. They add flexibility to homeowners who can, at some point, rent out the unit and then use it themselves. And, for me, one of the most beneficial aspects is that they allow families to live close—both younger members of the family and seniors.

I believe ADUs will continue to grow as a very positive, much needed type of residential construction. I know this book will be useful to you in your exploration of this new and exciting construction concept.

Below: For Hamilton Court redwood lattice screens were installed between the ADU and the master bedroom in the main house to provide privacy. Star Jasmine was planted on the lattice work, which will eventually cover the screens.

ACKNOWLEDGMENTS

I am always so grateful to the homeowners and architects who share their wonderful stories and great expertise. Their stories are inspiring, interesting, and educational. The beauty of this book is in large part due to the great expertise of the photographers who contributed their excellent work—I am very appreciative of all of them. Special thanks to my friend Art Gray for his extra effort with exceptional photos. Thank you to my dear friend Chuck Lockhart, who has created the beautiful graphics for this—and most of my other books—with amazing precision and going a million extra miles to help. And thanks to my friend Peter Chapman for his continued support. A major thanks to my editor, Madge Baird, who is so supportive of my work and makes my job so pleasant, and to the rest of the enthusiastic and professional team at Gibbs Smith—Kim Eddy, Virginia Snow, and Leslie Stitt. My love and gratitude to my husband, Rob, who is there for me in a million ways. Thank you also to my daughter, Alexandra; son, Jesse; and bonus child, Mella, who all cheer me on. These books are labors of love and I thank all the people who support these efforts.

ZUMETTE ADU

PANELIZATION

LOCATION: Mystic, Connecticut

PHOTOGRAPHER
Mark Bealer
Studio 66
www.studio66photography.com

DESIGNER/MANUFACTURER
Unity Homes
https://unityhomes.com

SIZE
790 square feet

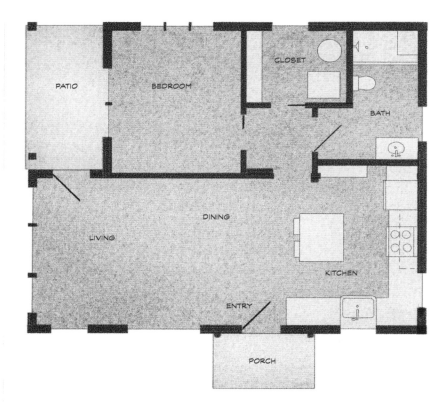

Richard and Ellen were living in the Hudson Valley, renting out their Mystic house on a short-term basis, and using the house themselves on occasion. Eventually they began to think about consolidating: building an ADU on the Mystic property to live in full-time, and continuing to rent out the main house. The ongoing rental income from the main house would make it possible for them to build the ADU. The main house would also allow them to host friends and family when it is not rented, effectively increasing their square footage when it was needed.

GREEN FEATURES

- Heat recovery ventilator
- All electric—no gas coming into the ADU
- Induction stove
- Quartz countertops

ENERGY FEATURES

- Air-source heat pump
- Solar panel ready
- Triple-pane windows
- Large overhangs
- Insulation exceeding code requirements
- Optimal orientation for solar gain in winter

BLOWER DOOR TEST

- .09 @ACH 50 (see sidebar on page 17)

BUILDING A NET ZERO ADU

The couple began looking for builders who had small house designs who could build a net zero ADU, which they wanted for its comfort and energy efficiency. They fell in love with the Zum design by Unity Homes and decided that was what they wanted to build. However, the Zum was a full-size house and would not meet the ADU 800-square-foot size limitations. Unity designers worked with the couple to customize the plan to meet their zoning and personal requirements. The couple was delighted with what became the Zumette, which met all their design and efficiency requirements.

Above: The clients hired a subcontractor to stain the concrete floor as they wanted a "warmer" look than that of typical sealed concrete. Because it is well insulated, the floor is comfortable for stocking feet, even in the winter.

RESEARCH AND DEVELOPMENT WITH THIS NEW DESIGN

While working on this new design, Unity decided to explore the use of some new materials and methods, teaming up with CertainTeed, a manufacturer of multiple construction products. The ADU was built using some materials that are nonstandard for Unity but are common in mainstream construction. For example, in their prefabricated panels, Unity used CertainTeed's blown fiberglass insulation instead of their usual cellulose. The owners were happy to have Unity do research and development with new products that would bring excellent energy use and comfort to their new ADU.

Below: The kitchen cabinets have a New England look in nautical navy. A botanical-bird print wallpaper adds an accent to the blue cabinets and a bit of whimsy to the open kitchen area. The single drawer dishwasher gives the owners the convenience of a dishwasher while maximizing cabinet space. The countertops and island top are quartz.

BUILDING AN ENERGY-EFFICIENT STRUCTURE

Sensors were installed throughout the structure to collect information on temperature, humidity, energy use, volatile organic compounds (VOC), and carbon dioxide emissions. According to project manager Beth Campbell, "The home is performing as modeled, which proves the credibility of the research and development assembly and materials that were used by Unity and CertainTeed teams." The data collected will be used to further improve the way that Unity Homes builds in the future.

Because the roof pitch direction on their Zumette is not optimal for solar panels, the couple plans to install a photovoltaic array on the existing garage that has a south-facing roof. They understand that their actual electrical use will depend on variables such as plug loads and HVAC settings, but they're expecting their PV system to produce sufficient power to serve the needs of their all-electric home.

The ADU has triple-pane windows to help maintain indoor temperature and an air-source heat pump, which is more energy efficient than a typical forced hot air system. A blower door test was performed (see sidebar on page 17) to find any leaks in the envelope of the ADU and patch them up. Because the ADU was built very tight, a heat recovery ventilator was installed to continuously exchange the stale interior air with the outside air, while not losing the heat or cool air already created in the ADU.

Right: The open floor plan, vaulted ceiling, and light-colored flooring make this space look larger than it is.

AN EASY SELECTION PROCESS

Richard and Ellen selected a package offered by Unity Homes that included a high-performance shell and a selection of finishes and fixtures. They opted to use Unity's standard offerings for engineered flooring, kitchen cabinets, plumbing fixtures, and siding, appreciating that they didn't have to go through the extensive research required to specify all the fixtures and finishes for their ADU.

The couple was able to keep costs down by utilizing a slab-on-grade foundation, building the ADU on a flat site that didn't require extensive excavation work, and choosing finishes that were beautiful but moderately priced.

Above: Horizontal shiplap panels add interest to this small bedroom.

QUICK CONSTRUCTION

Because the panels were prefabricated in the factory, the entire shell of this ADU was assembled in just a few snowy days. Richard and Ellen hired a local general contractor to prepare the site and install the insulated slab foundation. After the Unity crew assembled the shell on-site, the contractor completed the home during the following months.

To create a distinct outdoor living area in the backyard, which is separate from the vacation rental on the same lot, the clients hired a landscaper to transform the yard into a private space with a concrete patio, walkways, and native plants.

When the ADU was complete, Richard and Ellen were very pleased with the results, including the craftsmanship of the structure. Unity now offers the Zumette model as part of their Express or ready-to-build plans.

BLOWER DOOR TEST

A blower door test is a diagnostic tool used to measure the airtightness of a structure and to see if there are any leaks in it. Leaks in the exterior envelope of an ADU or house increase energy needs. To determine the extent of a structure's air leaks, professionals conduct a blower door test, in which a powerful fan is mounted into an exterior door opening and sealed tightly to the frame. During a depressurization test, the fan pulls air out of the house, lowering the interior pressure and pulling air in from the outside through unsealed cracks and openings. Gauges measure the difference between indoor and outdoor air pressure to calculate the air leakage rate and to identify where the leaks are; leaks are then sealed.

The test is then repeated. A common measure of this leakage is called "air changes per hour," or ACH, and represents the number of times the air inside a house is exchanged with outside air. This is measured at 50 Pascals, a measure of pressure. While an old house might have as many as 8 ACH, the Zumette ADU scored an impressive 0.9 ACH. More air changes mean leakier homes, higher fuel costs, and greater potential for moisture intrusion.

This test is required for certain certification programs, including ENERGY STAR and Passive House (Passivhaus). Passive House has the most stringent blower door test requirements, allowing a maximum infiltration of 0.6 air changes per hour (ACH) when measured at 50 Pascals pressure difference.

Properly sealing a house will increase comfort, reduce energy costs, and improve indoor air quality. Anyone thinking of buying an ADU or house should consider having a blower door test performed. To find certified contractors to perform a blower door test on your home, visit www.resnet.us.

SONOMA VALLEY A-FRAME

KIT HOME

LOCATION: Sonoma Valley, California

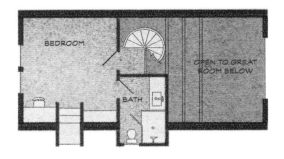

PHOTOGRAPHER
Jack Hecker, except where noted

ARCHITECT
Kerman & Morris Architects
www.kermanmorris.com

GENERAL CONTRACTOR
Atkinson Construction
www.atkn.com

MANUFACTURER
Avrame Kit Homes
https://avrame.com

SIZE
1,038 square feet

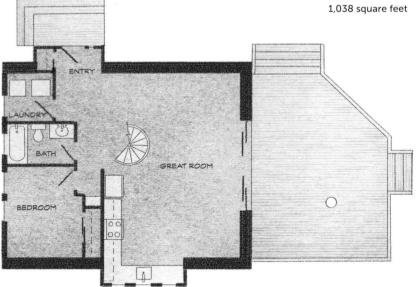

Ash and Debbie Notaney were looking for an investment property second home away from their current San Francisco home, but close enough to drive to. The couple love Sonoma County—Debbie having grown up there—and its proximity to the wineries. They sought land that had the potential to add an ADU so they could earn extra income and maximize the property.

Below: With the shape of the lot, the A-frame at 30 x 30 feet was the perfect fit. The house and deck were built to be both fire-resistant and sustainable with standing seam metal and fiber cement siding.

Searching online they happened on a Sonoma Valley property that had been on the market for a while and its price had just been reduced—so they jumped on it. An 800-square-foot log cabin was located on the property, so they decided to build the ADU to the maximum allowed by code and design it so that in the future they could make the ADU their primary home and rent out the cabin. After purchasing the property, they had to research how large the ADU could be with site constraints such as property lines, trees, underground pipelines, and a creek.

GREEN FEATURES
- Careful siting of ADU to avoid cutting down trees or impacting the creek
- Native landscaping
- Noncombustible fiber cement siding
- Recyclable metal roofing
- Permeable material for landscaping

ENERGY FEATURES
- High efficiency insulation
- Day lighting
- LED Lighting
- Mini-split heating/cooling
- Smart thermostat
- Solar panels
- Optimal solar orientation

Right: The beams crossing the open ceiling are part of the A-frame structure. They were supplied as raw, unattractive LVL (laminated veneer lumber) beams. Ash and Debbie carefully sanded and stained them. They say the stained beams work well with the white oak paneling they selected for the sloped ceilings.

FINDING A PREFAB OPTION

Having worked in the prefab industry years before, Ash preferred those methods rather than site building. Prefab construction, he believed, would allow them to build a unique, designed home more quickly than if it were built on-site.

They searched many different options, but most methods they looked at would create a rectangular footprint, and their site required a square footprint to maximize the use of the land. In addition, they wanted to keep as many of the mature trees on the land that they could. The A-frame kit they selected allowed them to build their home with a 30 x 30-foot footprint with minimal disturbance to the land. As a bonus, with this method they were able to add a second story and have high ceilings, which make the house feel more spacious. It took just six months for their house to be completed, and at a reasonable cost.

Without taking advantage of the prefab A-frame system, they say they would either have had to spend a lot more time and money or select a simpler design. Ash and Debbie plan to move into their ADU in about four years after their children have gone off to college.

Opposite: The deck off the kitchen is one of the several outdoor seating areas. The couple chose to retain as many trees as possible; one large live oak tree comes up through the outdoor deck.

Above: The couple designed the kitchen around the orange retro-style SMEG fridge, which they fell in love with. They say it also inspired the color pallet of the house.

MAXIMIZING THE SPACE

Because there is some potential for wasted space on the sides of the A-frame, the couple worked with their general contractor, as the building was going up, to find creative solutions to maximize the use of the space. They fit desks, storage cubbies, and an open closet into those areas around the periphery that would otherwise be wasted.

SPIRAL STAIRCASES

Spiral staircases are particularly useful in small houses since they take up far less space and can be tucked away in a corner of the room rather than dominating the space. These staircases are available for interior and exterior applications and can be prefabricated or custom designed in a variety of styles—from farmhouse to modern—and materials, from metal to wood. They also allow light to flow through them, an advantage in a small house where lots of light is essential in making the space feel larger.

The spiral stair in this house was key to maximizing their use of space, according to Ash and Debbie. Their spiral staircase takes up much less space than a regular flight of stairs and their kit staircase went together quickly. The most challenging aspect of their staircase was getting large furnishings up the stairs. The homeowners were alerted to this issue by the manufacturer, so they had some large items, such as the toilet and vanity unit, lifted before the staircase was installed. Another possible disadvantage when choosing this type of staircase can be the difficulty for physically challenged people and young children to maneuver the steep stairs. The cost of spiral staircases is dependent on the material used, its width, height, and cost of installation.

Opposite: The spiral staircase fits perfectly in this moderately sized ADU.

MAXIMIZING THE LIGHT

The couple put a great deal of effort into the lighting design. The ADU has several different types of dimmable lighting to provide different mood options: can lights for general lighting; pendants to highlight specific areas, such as the dining table; and lights on the upper surfaces of the beams to illuminate the ceiling, for soft indirect light.

There are several skylights throughout the house adding to the light provided by the many windows. An oversized sliding door in the kitchen area not only provides a good deal of light but also extends the living space of the house. A window leading out to a balcony from a bedroom brings in substantial light and provides additional beautiful views.

Above: The construction of the house with the beams, multiple windows, and white oak paneling adds to the beauty of the interior of the house.

Opposite top: With the height and orientation of the window and Juliet balcony in the upstairs bedroom, there is a great view of the Sonoma Mountains. The couple added the balcony as a fun element to view the surroundings.

Opposite bottom: This is one of two sleeping areas in the ADU. The owners found a "ladder" desk to provide a convenient working space and shelving.

Opposite top: An outdoor pergola, accessible to both houses, provides an additional dining area.

Opposite bottom: In the corner of the property is a beautiful, mature oak tree that the couple wanted to retain. They also thought a great use of the land by the tree would be a bocce court built around the base of the tree.

Above: This shows the house alongside the original log cabin, the container pool, the bocce court, and multiple outdoor living spaces.

ARGYLE ADU

SITE-BUILT

LOCATION: Washington, DC

PHOTOGRAPHER
Studio HDP
www.studiohdp.com

ARCHITECT
McInturff Architects
www.mcinturffarchitects.com

GENERAL CONTRACTOR
Acadia Contractors, Inc.
www.acadiacontractorsinc.com

STRUCTURAL ENGINEER
Norton Consulting Engineers
https://nortonengr.com

LANDSCAPE ARCHITECT
Lila Fendrick Landscape Architects
www.fendrickdesign.com

SIZE
ADU 712 square feet
House Addition 1,646 square feet

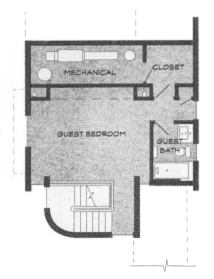

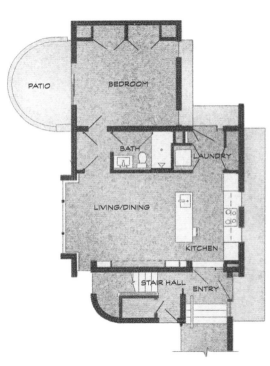

One of the main intents for establishing ADUs is so older parents can live close to family and age in place. This is the story of one such family, with the wife's retired father relocating to Washington, DC, from New Jersey.

The family decided to take advantage of recently revised District of Columbia zoning codes that now allow homeowners to build accessory dwelling units more easily on their properties. This provision is allowing many multigenerational families to be able to provide age-in-place housing for their older relatives, with reasonable access to urban amenities, without resorting to assisted living facilities.

Above: The house complex consists of a main house, an ADU, and a house addition. The two later parts are joined to the main house with a bridge connector.

GREEN FEATURES

- Quartz countertops
- Cement-based siding
- Low VOC finishes
- Energy recovery ventilator (ERV)
- No gas coming into the home
- Induction cooktop

ENERGY FEATURES

- Ceiling fans
- Super insulation
- Air-to-water heat pump system
- Radiant floor heating
- Solar ready

The owners were also hoping to add an addition to their main house. But the presence of a heritage tree in their rear yard, which is a protected species, limited their ability to do so. With McInturff Architects, they came up with a creative hybrid plan to build both an ADU and addition that would comply with local zoning laws. In addition to the self-sufficient accessory apartment on the lower level, they added a bedroom suite on the upper level that can act as a guest room or office for either the apartment or the house. The addition includes the bridge between the structures and the upper floor, which is a bedroom and bathroom. The bridge is lifted off the ground on piers so that it doesn't harm the tree or its roots and comfortably connects the two structures.

Opposite: A 30-foot bridge was designed to protect the root structure of an existing 40-foot oak tree and acts as a gallery space in which one can open two sets of sliding doors onto the rear yard, creating the feeling of an open breezeway. The bridge levels downward as the exterior grade elevation changes and terminates at the accessory apartment at the lower end of the site, allowing for easy accessibility.

Right: A small table and chairs in the open living area provide a place to eat. By having an open kitchen/living/dining space, a high-ceilinged bedroom, plenty of operable windows open to all orientations, and direct access to multiple outdoor spaces, the space feels loftier than it is.

Below: The open floor plan makes the ADU feel large with the light-colored white oak flooring, white porcelain tile flooring, and the many windows and doors bringing in an abundance of light.

TWO INDEPENDENT NEW HOUSING UNITS

The way the new ADU and addition were created, all three areas, including the main house, can be closed off for privacy, making the space flexible for several different living arrangements in the future not just for this family, but for other future owners and whatever their needs might be. There are multiple entrances to the ADU—from the driveway, the bedroom, and the bridge from the main house. The upstairs addition can also be accessed by a door on the bridge, without entering the ADU. With this configuration everyone's independence is preserved.

SUSTAINABILITY AND ENERGY EFFICIENCY AS PRIORITIES

Sustainability was a major factor in the design of the structure. The cement-based siding on the exterior of the ADU is resistant to weathering, rot, and pests, and the exterior windows are highly resilient aluminum-clad. Paints are water-based low-VOC, with colors that relate to the existing and adjacent houses. The white siding coordinates with the color of the existing main house and the red siding references the brick of the adjacent houses. The shingle roofing is expected to last thirty years, and the synthetic decking avoids the need to use increasingly scarce hardwoods like ipe.

Opposite: The upstairs addition includes a bedroom and bathroom that can be privately accessed through a door in the bridge or the entrance to the new addition. Clerestory windows (see sidebar on page 129) at the high point of the unit along with the other windows in the unit bring in a good deal of light.

Above: Steps ascend from the entrance hall of the new unit to the upper addition, which includes a bedroom and bathroom.

The addition is designed for responsible energy efficiency and comfort. The owner's father, who is an engineer, worked with the builder and architects to design a state-of-the-art HVAC system, which is both efficient and comfortable. The exterior walls have a layer of continuous insulation along the entire building envelope and are spray-foamed to attain an R-value greater than what is required by code. The mechanical system has no carbon gas coming into the house (see sidebar on page 37), and all the cooking appliances are electric. The heating and cooling requirements of the new spaces are provided by a high-efficiency air-to-water heat pump system that provides heating and cooling to three air handlers, heat for the in-slab radiant floor system in the accessory apartment, and heat for domestic hot water. A full-house dehumidifier, coupled with two energy recovery ventilators (ERVs), recaptures conditioned air and keeps inside air fresh year-round. The roof is also designed to support a future array of solar panels.

Above: The shape of the ADU and addition was partially influenced by the father's fond memories of the shape of his parents' home, which his mother had designed. There are multiple doors into the new section via the bridge, the entrance to the new unit, and several into the ADU itself.

WHY NO NATURAL GAS

Natural gas is used in homes for heating and cooling, and for gas stoves and ovens, fireplaces, laundry dryers, barbecue grills, and fire pits. But it is becoming increasingly popular for newer homes to be built without gas lines. Natural gas leaks can cause gas poisoning as well as fires and explosions. Some studies suggest that gas stoves emit significant levels of nitrogen dioxide, carbon monoxide, and fine particulate matter, which can rise to unsafe levels indoors without proper ventilation. Studies suggest that indoor gas stove usage is associated with an increased risk of asthma among children, and the volatile organic chemicals are known to be toxic when leaked.

Even when functioning properly, gas cooking appliances can lead to poor indoor air quality. Natural gas is considered bad for the environment since it pollutes the air, depletes the ozone layer, is a nonrenewable energy source, and contributes to warming the planet.

The Federal Inflation Reduction Act provides point-of-sale rebates for qualified high-efficiency electric appliances (such as heat pumps for space heating and cooling) for low- or moderate-income homes converting from gas to electric. Various places around the world are phasing out natural gas in homes, including areas of the UK, Europe, Canada, and the United States.

Above: This door into the bridge area provides an entrance to either the ADU or the upstairs addition, so either can be privately entered.

Opposite: This colorful entrance by the driveway provides a way to enter the house without steps, which works well for anyone physically challenged.

CANTERBURY ADU

SITE-BUILT

LOCATION: Austin, Texas

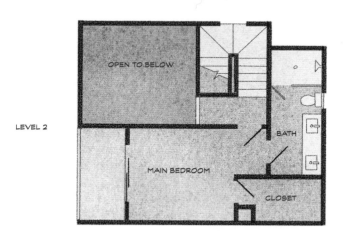

LEVEL 2

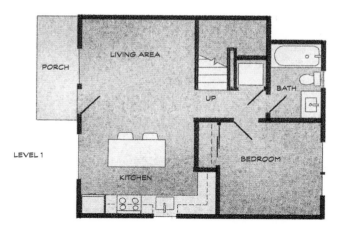

LEVEL 1

PHOTOGRAPHER
Andrea Calo
www.andreacalo.com

ARCHITECT
Point B
https://pbdesigngroup.com

GENERAL CONTRACTOR
Masterpiece Building of Austin
www.masterpieceaustin.com

SIZE
996 square feet

Opposite: The roof and siding on the exterior of the house are dark corrugated metal, which contrasts with the natural wood surrounding the second-floor front deck. Cut to size, metal panel siding reduces waste, does not require paint, and decreases required maintenance. Large strategically placed windows were used to maximize light coming into the house and reduce thermal load. The two-story unit has two bedrooms and two full bathrooms.

Christian Moreno, and his fiancée, Mary Rose Wight, were looking for a residence in Austin with additional property where he could build an ADU. They found a bungalow built around 1935, with the extra property they were seeking. The ADU was built to house visiting family and friends but also as a short-term rental property. Christian said it was the financial aspect of the ADU that was most enticing. Using the ADU as income property, he plans to be able to offset much of the cost of the main house. He wanted it to be very attractive and comfortable, not only for the renters but for his guests.

GREEN FEATURES

- Metal roofing and siding
- Quartz countertops
- WaterSense faucets
  and showerhead
- Xeriscaping
- Native plants
- Recycled materials
- Locally sourced materials

ENERGY FEATURES

- High efficiency insulation
- Strategically placed windows
- Ceiling fan
- LED lighting
- Concrete floors

Since Christian works from home, he was able to clearly communicate to the architects what design aspects should be incorporated into the ADU to make it work-at-home friendly for guests and renters. Many of the other decisions, such as sustainability and efficiency, he left up to the architects.

Above: The living area has an open concept with the living room area open to the kitchen. The concrete flooring required less building materials and also functions as thermal mass to help regulate the interior temperature.

Opposite: The playfully colored kitchen with its locally produced blue custom cabinets and bright Elisa Pisano cement tile backsplash contrasts beautifully with the darker exterior of the house. The countertops are quartz.

BRINGING POINT B ON BOARD

Through an acquaintance, Christian met the architects at Point B. He was impressed by their portfolio online and, upon meeting them, felt they had "good energy." He told them what he wanted in the design and says they were wonderful at conceptualizing his vision. Christian hopes to build future homes and ADUs, and he would happily work with the crew at Point B again.

Above: A covered deck is off the second-floor primary bedroom. The wood panels contrast with the metal siding and railings.

Opposite: High cathedral ceilings expand the feel of the primary bedroom. The ceiling fan provides cool breezes, without using the air-conditioning.

THE DESIGN

The architects at Point B worked not only to make the house attractive, but also to make it efficient and low maintenance. The corrugated metal roofing and siding are highly sustainable, requiring minimal maintenance over future years. According to Point B architect Maggie Wylie, "Austin's energy code and building requirements are 'green' by nature so with everything we design, sustainability (to an extent) is built-in. There are requirements on envelope design, insulation, window code, low-flow faucets, etc. Energy efficiency was not a driving force but a baked-in standard that we design to daily."

The walls and roof were insulated with spray foam, so the envelope is highly efficient. The plumbing fixtures are all low-flow and WaterSense certified (see sidebar on page 47). Wylie says the biggest objective in making design decisions were life-cycle costs of materials and maintenance. The roof and siding have a twenty-year warranty, removing any need for repainting in the next twenty years. The materials, such as the metal siding and roofing and the concrete floors, are very durable and low maintenance. The HVAC is highly efficient for effective cooling and heating.

Christian is an IT professional and looks forward to investing in future properties as an additional avocation.

Above: The main bathroom has double sinks and quartz countertops. The barrier-free walk-in shower (see sidebar on page 219) is tiled from floor to ceiling with terra cotta tiles. The white walls have a glazed finish.

WATERSENSE

WaterSense® is a voluntary water-efficiency program and a label the U.S. Environmental Protection agency (EPA) allows companies to use on products that have been independently certified to conform to WaterSense specifications for efficiency and performance. Products that bear this label are proof for consumers that the product was tested and meets EPA criteria for water efficiency and performance. As an example, according to WaterSense, "by replacing a showerhead with a WaterSense-labeled model, the average family can save more than 2,700 gallons of water each year." Products that can qualify for the WaterSense label include bathroom sink faucets, showerheads, toilets, flushing urinals, and outdoor spray sprinkler bodies. For additional information, see the U.S. EPA's website (www.epa.gov/watersense).

CLAYTON STREET ADU

PANELIZED

LOCATION: Denver, Colorado

PHOTOGRAPHER
Zachary Cornwell
www.zacharycornwellphotography.com

ARCHITECT/PANEL MANUFACTURER
Simple Homes
www.simplehomes.com

GENERAL CONTRACTOR
L & D Construction
https://ldconstructiondenver.com

SIZE
350 square feet

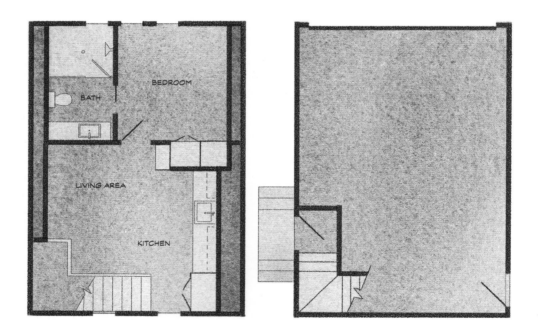

Opposite: The ADU sits on the alley behind the main house. The siding of the ADU is pre-stained cedar vertical shiplap designed to mimic rustic barnwood. The siding is over a rainscreen that should allow the wood to last for over 100 years.

Jeffrey Hopfenbeck (a co-owner of Simple Homes) and his wife, Linnea, decided to build this ADU as they prepared to have their first child. Their families live out of town; Linnea's family lives in Washington, Jeffrey's in the mountains of Colorado. Jeffrey and Linnea wanted to have space for their family and friends to visit and stay for extended periods of time. While the couple love their house, a shotgun-style Victorian that was built in 1886, it is quite small, and they recognized it would not be the best for long-term family visits.

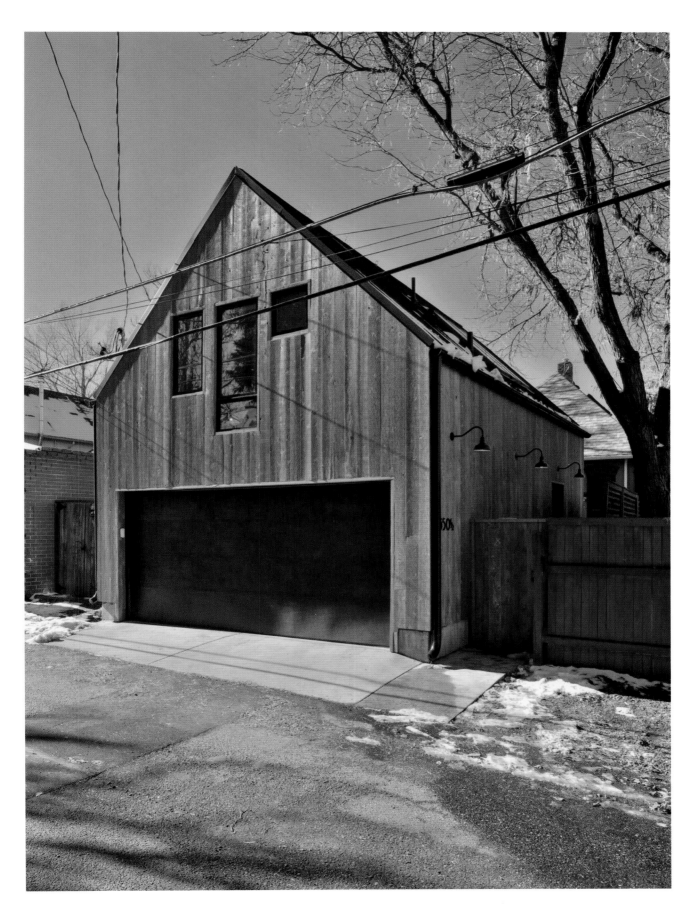

GREEN FEATURES

- No gas coming into the house
- Framing waste was reduced 15 percent compared to on-site construction

ENERGY FEATURES

- Continuous insulation to reduce thermal bridging
- Heat pump HVAC

GOALS IN DESIGNING THE HOUSE

The couple had three primary design goals in designing the ADU. They wanted to maximize the space on their tiny urban lot, while adhering to the tight zoning constraints that limited height and floor area. The structure had to be highly efficient to construct in terms of time, cost, and materials. And they wanted to create a building that is both contemporary and blends seamlessly into the overall urban fabric of their historic neighborhood.

Above: Large skylights were added to highlight the large tree in the neighbor's yard. A substantial amount of light from the skylights also makes the space feel light and airy. The drop-leaf table provides a place for two or more people to dine.

Opposite Top: High ceilings and light-colored walls make the common space look much bigger. The ceiling design has exposed trusses and painted pine tongue-and-groove paneling.

Opposite Bottom: The kitchen includes a refrigerator, sink, undercounter dishwasher, and lots of storage space.

THE PETITE DESIGN

The 350-square-foot ADU was designed to fit the narrow lot behind the Victorian home. As there are alleys throughout the city, most ADUs, in Denver, are built in the carriage house or laneway form like this one. This tiny footprint includes a full one-bedroom apartment with living, dining, kitchen, laundry, bedroom, and bath.

Left: A mini-split unit keeps the entire unit cool in the summer and warm in the winter.

Opposite: White walls and cabinetry and light hickory wire-brushed engineered hardwood flooring make this room feel spacious.

BUILDING WITH PANELIZATION

The house was built using a prefab building system that included wall panels and attic trusses. According to Hopfenbeck, Simple Homes delivers wall panels with a higher level of finish than most panelized construction companies. Typically, wall panels are delivered with framing, sheathing, weather barrier, and windows preinstalled—allowing homes to go from foundation to weathertight in one day. With this project, continuous exterior insulation was also preinstalled in the factory to improve energy efficiency.

Simple Homes designers also focused on applying the latest design technology and principles with a design software, Design for Manufacture and Assembly (DfMA), a program that avoids costly mistakes in the early stages of product modeling that could complicate and delay the manufacturing process and sustainability goals. They use this program to increase speed and reduce costs. Simple Homes projects start with the development of a full "digital twin," a virtual replica of the project that includes every part and piece in the building. The data in this model is then run through a variety of internally developed algorithms to help optimize for material waste, labor hours, and energy performance.

According to Hopfenbeck, the overall result is substantial time savings (50–70 percent), meaningful material waste reduction (10–15 percent), and cost savings (10–15 percent), compared to a traditional stick-frame build.

MAKING GREAT
USE OF THE SPACE

Now that the ADU is completed, Hopfenbeck says they love the flexibility the space affords. Since their son was born in August they have had a steady stream of family visitors. They have been able to host extended visits from family while also still ensuring that everyone has their own space to recharge and relax. When it has not been occupied by family, the couple has used the space almost every day—either as extra office space, with Linnea working from home, as an additional living area for fun family movie nights, or as a short-term rental.

Opposite: The bathroom sink is a modern rectangular, with a lighted mirror above.

Above: The shower is tiled with white hex tile on the floor and dark green subway tile on the walls, with a small window well situated for privacy.

Left: Multiple skylights make this room feel more spacious, and they add a substantial amount of light into the entire area.

Opposite: The cozy sitting area also provides extra sleeping space when several people are guests at the unit.

SKYLIGHTS

Skylights can be a great addition to a particularly small house because they don't take away from wall space while allowing in light, solar energy, and natural ventilation. They come in a variety of configurations—some that cannot open and others that can be opened manually or with a remote control. Many are available with shades, so they can limit the entrance of light, when that is preferable. Skylights can add value to a home with their energy savings and their attractive presentation. Older models tended to leak when water got under the flashing; newer models are less prone to leak if installed properly. The skylights in the Clayton Street ADU are by Velux, which offers a solar-powered rain sensor and a no-leak warranty.

FERN STREET ADU

SITE-BUILT

LOCATION: Atlanta, Georgia

PHOTOGRAPHER
Erik Meadows
www.erikmeadows.com

DESIGNER/BUILDER
ATL ADU CO
www.atladuco.com

GENERAL CONTRACTOR
Expert Renovations, LLC
http://renovationsgroup.net

SIZE
ADU 645 square feet
Porch 104 square feet

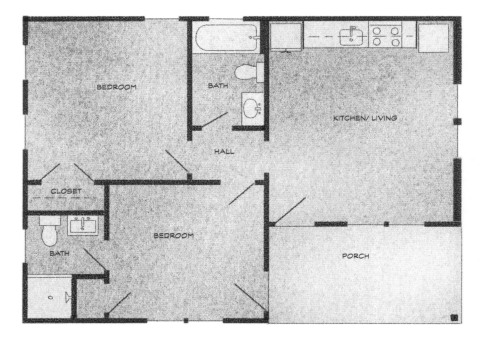

After running the Porter Beer Bar in Atlanta for fourteen years, Molly Gunn and her husband, Nick Rutherford, decided to sell the business, since the pandemic made it too difficult to continue. Earlier, in 2017, they had begun investing in real estate as a vehicle for their retirement. They purchased six single-family houses to rent. As the market turned in 2021, they did not purchase any more investment properties but chose to use their existing properties to

Below: The ADU matches the aesthetic of the primary house and the surrounding neighborhood. Both the primary and secondary units are long-term rentals, so they separated utilities on this project rather than tying the ADU into the main house. The design is inspired by Atlanta's abundance of American Craftsman bungalows. The siding is fiber cement.

GREEN FEATURES

- Low-flow toilets
- Natural landscaping
- Storm water management

ENERGY FEATURES

- High efficiency insulation
- Mini-split heat pump
- LED lights
- Ceiling fans

increase their cash flow. In 2022 they built their first ADU on one of their rental properties. There was so much demand to rent these properties, they have now completed their second ADU and are in the process of building a third. Gunn says ADUs provide a safe way for them to add on to the properties they already own, and they are confident this will produce cash flow and be an excellent business decision.

CHOOSING A BUILDER

The couple says working with ATL ADU was a huge convenience. The company worked directly with the contractor and was able to easily get through the permitting process in the City of Atlanta. They were pleased not to have to interact with the city on their own.

Gunn says she has not seen any other ADU designs that she thought were as beautiful as those provided by ATL ADU. She particularly likes the spacious feeling of the unit despite its small size. She opted to build her second (now complete) and third units with the company because of the high quality she saw with their first ADU.

Unlike some other ADU builders, ATL ADU offers predesigned models instead of custom designs. Gunn and Rutherford prefer this type of company because they feel it is an efficient and cost-saving way to build. (See sidebar on page 65.)

Left: A kitchen and living room open onto a deep covered porch.

Below: Flooring throughout most of the ADU is red oak engineered hardwood. A cafe table in the open common area provides a place to eat. The pitched ceiling makes this open area feel larger than it is.

HOW THE ADU IS USED

Gunn says since it is cost prohibitive for many people to rent a single-family home in the City of Atlanta, ADUs provide a good option. The couple looks for long-term renters for all their properties so they can have an ongoing relationship with them. From their experience they say that renters who want to live in an ADU are often those who need a yard for their pets and those that desire privacy, with no shared walls. Some renters, such as those in the medical field, work swing or night shifts, and need to sleep during the day. ADUs address the needs for many people who find that apartment or condo dwelling doesn't fit their lifestyle.

Above: The high set window in the main bathroom provides lots of light while still providing privacy.

Opposite: Double windows in the main bedroom provide a good deal of natural light and ventilation.

Above: The second bedroom was set up to function as a work area.

CUSTOM-DESIGNED VS PREDESIGNED ADU MODELS

Some companies will custom design any ADU that the customer requests. Some of these are meant to imitate the main house and some have special requirements, such as a workspace or play area. Custom-designed units allow the consumer to have any type of configuration and design within the confines of the municipality's restrictions. These units will be specifically designed by an independent architect or by the builder or manufacturer.

Other companies such as ATL ADU CO offer a variety of plans from which the homeowner can select. There are several advantages to buying this type of unit. A predesigned model means less back-and-forth between the architect and the homeowner, which translates to less time and money spent on the project. Since the builder has constructed this unit in the past, it provides a more efficient and speedy construction process and less lead time on custom materials. There are currently some local governments that are fast-tracking predesigned ADUs for interested customers—helping them avoid the wait time of an individual approval process. An example of this can be seen in the South Sound ADU in this book. Preapproved plans for this ADU were designed for the City of Olympia Housing Authority by The Artisans Group. Under the Standard Plan Program in Los Angeles; as an example, permits can be processed in a day instead of weeks.

PLYMOUTH ADU

SITE-BUILT

LOCATION: Los Angeles, California

PHOTOGRAPHER
Art Gray
http://artgrayphotography.com

ARCHITECT
Vertebrae
www.vertebrae.la

GENERAL CONTRACTOR
Rock Construction & Management, Inc.
www.rockconstruction.com

SIZE
370 square feet

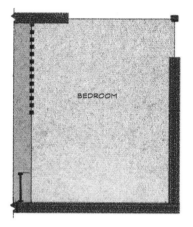

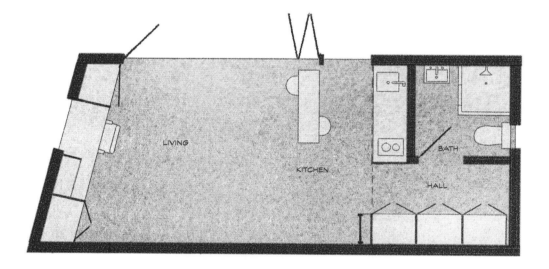

Opposite: The exterior of the ADU has fiber cement siding with a cool roof, that is not generally visible. The bifold glass doors open the ADU to a luxurious outdoor sitting area, pool, and barbecue. The asymmetrical butterfly roof expands the apparent dimension of the main living area despite the very small footprint and provides for a sleeping loft on one end of the building and plentiful built-in storage on the other.

When homeowners Leslie-Anne Huff and Reggie Panaligan were expecting their first child, they decided they wanted to expand their living space with an ADU. The extra space would provide them with a "multiuse retreat"—a guest house, pool house, and workspace.

Prior to the construction of the ADU, the home-owners had a carport at the rear of the lot. It was being used primarily for storage, rather than for parking. The couple wanted a structure with flexible use that could also store their things out of sight. When the ADU was completed, the built-in closets and cabinets function as storage space for the main house. Reggie also works there two days a week and Leslie-Anne, an actress, uses the space to tape her auditions.

GREEN FEATURES
- Materials with recycled content
- Fiber cement siding

ENERGY FEATURES
- Cool roof
- High efficiency windows
- Cement floors
- Mini-split heat pump
- Tankless water heater
- LED lights
- High efficiency insulation

Left: Large, glass bifold doors allow for a seamless connection to the outdoors and fill the interior with lots of natural light. The finished floor is ceramic tile installed over a concrete slab-on-grade foundation.

A DESIGN PLAN

The couple's main house is a hundred-year-old-plus Windsor-style home. Because their house is so classic, they chose to design the ADU with a modern aesthetic. They view the ADU as the twenty-first-century "sister" to their main house. They chose Vertebrae to design their structure because they admired their portfolio of existing ADU projects, and they also felt "a strong creative connection" to the principal of Vertebrae, Lisa Little.

The couple wanted their ADU to have great indoor/outdoor flow and be in sync with the main house. The structure had to be flexible and with space to store their belongings. According to project manager, Jesse Chappelle, "Throughout the ADU, every formal move and architectural element from the scale of the building to furniture and finish was designed to contribute to an atmosphere of lightness and usability without impeding circulation."

The ADU includes everything needed to function as an additional living space for a multigenerational family or as a stand-alone dwelling: a kitchen, full bath, built-in desk, storage, living space, and a sleeping loft.

Below: The loft is accessed by a wall-mounted ladder and is enclosed with wood slats that delineate space without dividing the overall volume.

Opposite: Looking down from the loft, the entire open area of the ADU can be seen.

ENERGY EFFICIENCY AS A PRIORITY

The couple say it was very important to ensure that the ADU was energy efficient. They connected the solar panels, previously built on the roof of the main house, to the ADU's system. The slab-on-grade foundation with tile stores the cool nighttime air and reduces the need for air-conditioning during the day. It was also an affordable and durable construction option in this climate. Energy-efficient systems were used including a mini-split heat pump and tankless water heater. The cool roof system (see sidebar on page 73) and high-performance insulation help to keep the interior at a comfortable temperature.

The abundance of glazing was designed to create a strong connection between the interior and exterior as well as offer plentiful natural daylighting and ventilation. Placing most of the glazing on the north side of the house in combination with high performance glass provides ample daylighting throughout the year while reducing heat gain in the hot summer months. All this creates a space that consumes less energy, is full of natural sunlight, doesn't get too hot in the summer, and allows the inhabitants to open the large bifold doors and enjoy the fresh air.

Above left: The powder-coated steel island was custom designed for the space and provides an eating area in the small kitchen. The ADU has two full walls of storage, one by the kitchen and another incorporated with the desk.

Above right: An LED-lit mirror, small sink, and tiled shower make up this petite bathroom.

COOL ROOFS

Cool roofs reflect the sun's radiation and emit absorbed heat back into the atmosphere. There are two criteria for cool roofs—solar reflectance [SR] (the ability of a surface to reflect solar radiation) and thermal emittance [TE] (the ability of the roof's surface to radiate absorbed solar energy). These roofs remain cooler and reduce the amount of heat that is transferred to the house below it, decreasing cooling costs and increasing comfort for the occupants. Cool roofs reduce stress on the roof, extending its life, and can also possibly qualify for rebates. The downside to cool roofs is they can reduce heat transmission to the house in colder months, increasing the need for mechanical heating. The Cool Roof Rating Council (CRRC) offers a directory of the solar reflectance and thermal emittance of over 3,000 rated roofing products. To calculate the savings by area, check the on-line calculator of Oak Ridge National Laboratory.

There are a variety of materials that can produce a cool roof. These perform best on flat roofs and those with low pitches. Low-pitch roofs are not as visible as high-pitched ones and may include some materials that are not as visually appealing as those used on high pitches. Some examples include single-ply membranes, built-up roofs, modified bitumen sheet membranes, and spray polyurethane foam roofs. High-pitched roofs can have cool roofs with such possibilities as asphalt shingles that are light colored or have a cool-colored granule surface, wood shingles, or metal shingles coated with cool-colored paint or have reflective mineral granules. Standing seam metal roofs and green roofs can be used on low- and high-pitched roofs. The cool roof on the Plymouth ADU is a cap sheet with reflective granules. A cap sheet consists of an upper layer of multilayer roofing system that covers and protects the layers below it and provides color, protection from fire, ultraviolet (UV) radiation protection, and resistance to mechanical abuse. The roof by CertainTeed on this ADU is 100 percent opaque to UV radiation.

SUNFLOWER ADU
STRUCTURAL INSULATED PANELS (SIPS)

LOCATION: Saint Paul, Minnesota

PHOTOGRAPHER
Alyssa Lee Photography
www.alyssaleephotography.com

ARCHITECT
Christopher Strom Architects
https://christopherstrom.com

GENERAL CONTRACTOR
Uber Built
www.uberbuilt.com

SIZE
780 square feet

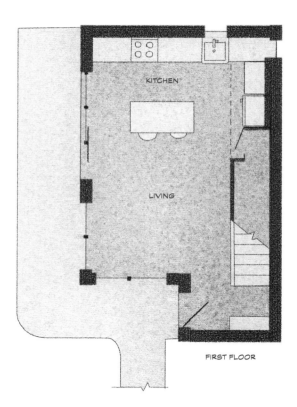

FIRST FLOOR

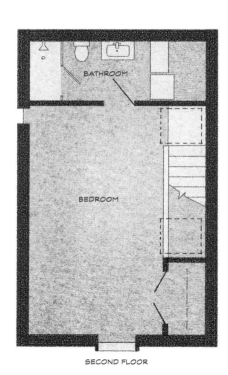

SECOND FLOOR

Opposite: The ADU was named Sunflower for its cheery yellow exterior. Although a bright color, it is surprisingly well hidden from the street view because of its location tucked behind the main home. Siding is engineered wood.

While teaching a pre-architecture course at his St. Olaf College alma mater, architect Christopher Strom met Isaiah Scharen, an undergraduate art student. So impressed with his work, Strom offered Isiah a summer internship at his firm.

The ADU design ideas emerged while Sonja, her two sons, and their partners were living together in their main house on the property during the pandemic. Isaiah and his partner, Maura, started dreaming

GREEN FEATURES

- No gas coming into the house
- Energy recovery ventilator (ERV)
- Recycled glass surfaces
- Sustainably harvested wood

ENERGY FEATURES

- SIPs
- Ceiling fan
- Solar panel ready
- Concrete floors
- Mini-split heating/cooling
- Hydronic radiant floors
- LED lights

BLOWER DOOR TEST

- 1.71 @ ACH 50 (see sidebar on page 17)

up and drafting plans for an ADU on the property using Saint Paul's new citywide ordinance for ADU construction. Sonja liked the initial ideas so much that she reached out to Christopher Strom and his associate architect Eric Johnson at Christopher Strom Architects to continue the ideas and details for the ADU. The project aligned well with the firm's emphasis on the latest technology, thoughtful use of materials, and efficient design along with beautiful aesthetics.

As the design developed during the pandemic gloom, they decided to name it the Sunflower and painted the exterior a cheerful yellow. The interior is filled with sunlight and pops of colors with the sage green kitchen cabinetry and artistic shower tile.

BUILDING EFFICIENTLY

While Isaiah was designing the ADU with Chris's firm, the cost of wood was going up. SIPs seemed like a great alternative when comparing their cost with that of traditional framing. Isaiah has become increasingly interested in using alternative materials that are cost effective, which also makes them more affordable overall. SIP Construction (see sidebar on page 79) was chosen not only for its cost efficiency but

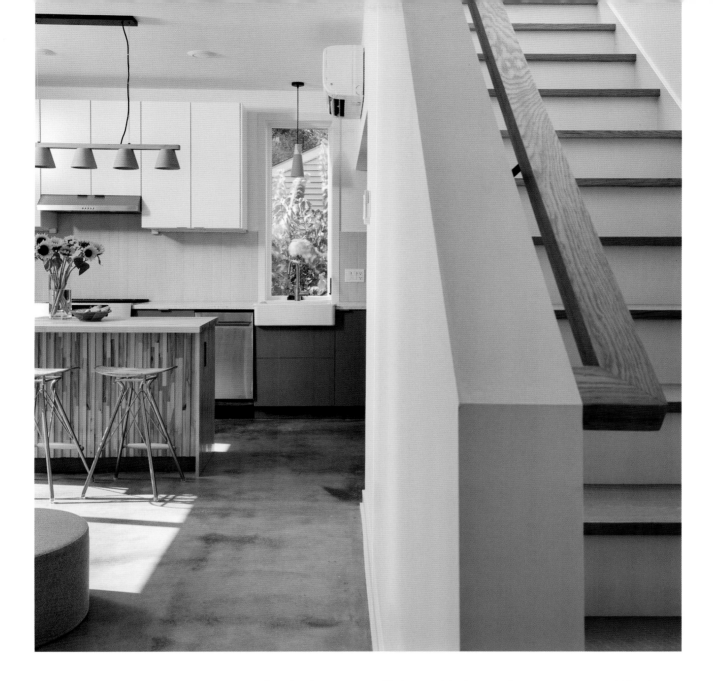

Opposite: One mini-split unit provides heat and cooling to supplement the radiant heating system on the first floor.

Above: The staircase leads to the sleeping loft and bathroom above.

also for its energy efficiency. Mother and son were especially drawn to the airtight, continuous insulation, and the SIPs' ability to limit construction waste. The noise resistance provided by SIPs was an additional benefit because of the ADU's urban location.

They aimed to make the house as energy efficient as possible. A highly efficient mini-split unit was installed to provide heat and air-conditioning. Hydronic radiant heating is installed within the concrete floors to help keep the house comfortable year-round. The concrete floors also serve as a thermal mass, meaning that the concrete stores heat from the natural light that passes through the windows. This heat then helps warm the ADU, especially in the cold Minnesotan winters.

SUSTAINABLE + HEALTHY OPTIONS SELECTED

The exterior of the ADU is clad in engineered siding, which provides a low maintenance, environmentally friendly alternative, reducing the carbon footprint. It is a composite material manufactured using wood veneers, scrap wood, and wood fibers bound with adhesives. Engineered wood is typically durable, resistant to moisture, and strong.

To keep the house healthy there is no gas coming into the house—all appliances are electric. There is also an energy recovery ventilator to remove stale air from the house and replace it with fresh outside air.

Above: The petite living room is open to the kitchen and dining area. The exposed concrete flooring serves as both the structural slab and the finished floor, which is an efficient use of the material, limiting waste. The concrete floors function as thermal mass helping to regulate the interior temperature.

Opposite: The sliding glass door opens to the outdoor patio that expands the living space. The large door and multiple windows provide natural light and ventilation.

STRUCTURAL INSULATED PANELS

Structural insulated panels (SIPS) are panels that are manufactured by sandwiching foam insulation between two outer structural panels (usually oriented strand board or plywood, or even metal). The panels are mechanically connected, like Lego pieces, limiting the possibility for air infiltration. SIPs can be custom designed for a particular house in dimensions as big as 8 x 24 foot (by comparison, standard plywood sheets are 4 x 8 foot). SIPs are increasingly popular for building walls, roofs, floors, and even foundations because of their strength, short construction time, low waste, and excellent insulating qualities. In a house built using SIPs, the heating, ventilation, and air-conditioning (HVAC) equipment is scaled down to save money, while the house stays comfortable with lower energy costs. SIPs also limit outside noise. To learn more, visit.sips.org.

CREATING A PUBLIC SPACE AND A PRIVATE "NEST"

Whereas ADUs are sometimes built above the garage, Sonja and Isaiah opted to build it free-standing so they could dedicate the lower level as well as the second floor for living space. The first floor has the gathering spaces, including the kitchen and living room, which opens to the out-side garden area. There are several south-facing large windows, which ease the heating burden while also connecting the residents with the out-doors. Sonja describes the upstairs area with the bedroom, bathroom, and laundry as the "nest." It has smaller windows and includes skylights that focus on sky and treetops rather than the more public outside area.

Isaiah currently lives in the ADU, but in the future, other family members plan to reside there. As she envisions many different chapters of communal living and various people enjoying the space, Sonja doesn't eliminate the possibility of living there her-self someday. This project has been a springboard for Isaiah to explore energy efficient and sustain-able architectural design as he moves from archi-tectural school to the workplace. His plans will continue to include designing ADUs that are built with high performance materials, are energy effi-cient and sustainable, all with an attempt to bring down costs.

Opposite top: Since many people now work from home, a work area with a desk is provided on the far side of the loft. One can see the many possibilities someone might use this area for in the future—such as a music room, a library, a TV room, and so on.

Opposite bottom: Several windows, including the skylight (see sidebar on page 57), and the open space overlooking the lower level provide ample light to this upper level. The ceiling fan helps to create a cool breeze.

Above: The upstairs shower was another area chosen for a pop of color. Sonja laid out the colors and wanted it to look like a Southwest sunrise.

PARKWAY LANEWAY

STRUCTURAL INSULATED PANELS (SIPS)

LOCATION: Vancouver, British Columbia

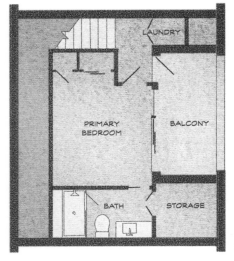

SECOND FLOOR

PHOTOGRAPHER
Martin Knowles
www.mkphotomedia.com

ARCHITECT
Nick Bray Architecture
https://nickbray.ca

GENERAL CONTRACTOR
Forte Projects
http://forteprojects.ca

SIZE
915 square feet

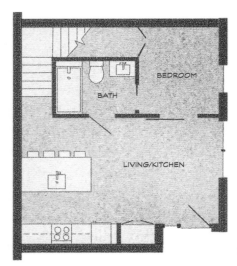

MAIN FLOOR

With the housing shortage and affordability issue in Vancouver, architect Nick Bray opted to build a spec house and accessory dwelling unit that would maximize the use of space on the lot and bring income for the potential owner. To maximize the density on each lot, Bray designed the main four-bedroom house with a one-bedroom "lock-off" suite below that could easily be part of the house as an office area, additional family rooms, or guest suite. There is also a two-bed, two-bath separate suite below the main

Below: The exterior of the ADU is a combination of metal, natural cedar, and fiber cement siding, which replicates the look of the main house and is low maintenance and durable. Metal roofing provides longevity and low maintenance. On the main house's east wall and the laneway's south wall, metal is continued down the facade to ground level, which Bray says is "practical and artistic." Overhangs around the periphery of the laneway reduce solar gain in the summer.

house. Both basement suites have private sunken patios. In addition, there is a two-bed, two-bath laneway situated behind the main house.

The occupants of the main house can make significant rental income from the other units to assist with their mortgage payments. To provide adequate separation and privacy between the different homes, each unit has its own entrance and outdoor area, as well as soundproof concrete walls and floors between them. Each unit is designed to be very space efficient, with no corridors or nonfunctional space. Bray says, "It's all about getting the most out of each parcel of land."

GREEN FEATURES
- Heat recovery ventilator
- Low VOC materials and finishes
- Induction stove
- Materials selected for longevity
- Metal roofing
- Composite flooring

ENERGY FEATURES
- SIPs
- High efficiency appliances
- Radiant floor heating
- Super insulation
- Heat pump for heating and cooling

CERTIFICATION
- Built Green Platinum Certification

Right: The eating bar/island provides comfortable seating for four people when entertaining or for just the residents when they are home alone. Although space is limited, there are full-sized appliances, including an induction cooktop, making it very workable for the residents.

OBJECTIVES IN THE DESIGN

When designing the house and additional dwellings, Bray says his main objective was to maximize the density and space efficiency of each unit to take the best advantage of the site. While increasing the potential rental income to assist with the housings' affordability, he also tried to design the main house to feel like an independent, high-end home. As with all his projects, Bray's other objective was to make the units as energy efficient as possible. Toward this end, he designed the house with SIPs, which are energy efficient and fast to install. He also used a highly efficient heating system and high efficiency windows. Since Vancouver, like most of the West Coast, is at high risk for earthquakes, the building's structure has also been reinforced to resist a significant quake.

Above: The frosted-glass barn door leads from the living room to the flex space that can be used as a guest room or home office. For entertaining, the barn door can be opened, almost doubling the first-floor space.

Opposite: The double-height ceiling above the staircase extends along the north edge of the kitchen, increasing its volume. That area of the kitchen is open to the skylight on the second-floor ceiling, bringing in light and expanding the feeling of space in the kitchen area. Bonus storage in the open space above the kitchen is accessed with a drop-down ladder.

Opposite top: The balcony off the main bedroom provides a nice place to relax but also brings in a good deal of light and, when the sliding door is open, natural ventilation.

Opposite bottom: The steeply gabled roofline cleverly adds bonus interior spaces to the upper floor with bench seating in the wide shower, extra width for the bed, and a built-in laundry with a stacked washer/dryer at the foot of the stairs. A black feature wall in the shower matches the slate tile flooring.

Above: The upper-level en suite, with a skylight, includes the primary bedroom and bathroom and opens to a private balcony overlooking a park.

DEALING WITH ZONING BYLAWS

Bray says the zoning bylaws for laneways in Vancouver are incredibly complicated and rigorous. He sought to design the units in a way to gain the most area he could with the exemptions that are allowed. This means using space that doesn't have to be included in the square-foot calculations, but still meets the requirements of the zoning laws. As an example, the house was recessed into the site, with four steps down to the front door, to allow for more height and space on the upper floor. Bray says every square inch is functional space, including the storage area that can be added on.

Above: The main house has two possible rental spaces beneath it.

In building these units Bray wanted to provide everything the homeowners would need, at a reasonable cost, since affordability is a major problem in Vancouver. He says these spaces function extremely well in spite of the fact that the space is limited and the materials used were affordable.

LANEWAY HOUSES

Laneway Houses are small-scale, fully independent homes that are typically built in the backyard of an existing single-family home where a garage once stood, just off the rear alley, or lane, hence the name laneway. There are rear alleys in several locations in Canada (North Vancouver, Calgary, Winnipeg, Edmonton, Ottawa, Toronto, Halifax) as well as some areas of the United States (Seattle, Portland, California). Laneways are a subcategory of accessory dwelling units (ADUs), which can also include basement dwellings, apartments over a garage, and additional houses on an existing lot where a house already exists. There are rules for laneway houses on their setback, space between the main house and laneway, maximum height, parking requirement, outdoor space, placement of windows and so on, depending on their location and local zoning laws. Regulations for all these units are specified by the local government, province, or state where they exist. As a result of the laneway boom, the lane areas in some locations, which previously were often neglected, have become revitalized while providing expanded housing options. This type of construction has added density to communities without construction of multistory apartment houses. Laneways, like other ADUs, offer an alternative type of housing for people who do not want to live in an apartment building, cannot afford or do not need a full-size, single-family house, or are looking for added income.

BEECH HAUS ADU

RENOVATION

LOCATION: Portland, Oregon

PHOTOGRAPHER
Christopher Dibble Photography
www.christopherdibble.com

DESIGNER
Dyer Studio, Inc.
www.dyerstudioinc.com

GENERAL CONTRACTOR
Owen Gabbert LLC
http://owengabbertllc.com

SIZE
400 square feet

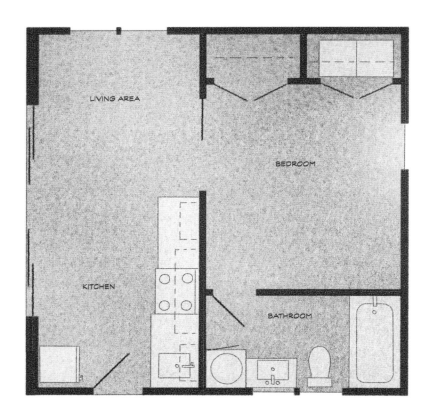

As an urban planner, homeowner Jodi Jacobson-Swartfager was pleased to be able to maximize the urban amenities in this vibrant area of Portland by building an ADU. She and her husband Jeff owned a small house in the Boise-Eliot neighborhood, located two blocks from the bustling Williams Avenue Business District, with plentiful eateries, shops, and an active destination. Their home was just a ten-minute bike ride into downtown. This made it feel like the ideal location to attract short-term rentals for an ADU.

Below: The Beech Haus was converted from a prefabricated garage. The siding is fiber cement, which needs minimal maintenance. An abundance of light comes into the ADU via large double sliding glass doors. Outdoor living space is provided in the front and the private side patios.

GREEN FEATURES
- Recycled materials on structure and oven

ENERGY FEATURES
- Mini-split heating/cooling
- Concrete floors

While studying for her master's degree in urban and regional planning at Portland State University, Jodi met several other students with knowledge in the design and construction of small structures—which she says planted the seed for utilizing her own backyard space. Through her diligent networking, she connected with designer Stephanie Dyer and contractor Owen Gabbert.

Jodi and Jeff had previously decided that their once-comfortable house on the property would be too small when children joined their family. But they love the home and the neighborhood and would one day like to return after their kids go off to college, so they decided to move into a larger home and rent out their smaller house. They then began thinking how they could maximize the livable space in that smaller home with an ADU on the property.

Above: The ceiling trusses and the wainscoting in the kitchen give the area a cozy, beachy ambiance. A small café table provides a place to comfortably dine in this light-filled area.

Opposite: The door between the bedroom and bathroom is a pocket door which expands the small space. Flooring throughout the ADU is a water-based epoxy on the original concrete that was ground down.

BUILDING THE ADU

Jodi and Jeff wanted an addition to their house to create passive income. Representatives of Owen Gabbert met with them several times to evaluate their development options for the property. They explored the possibilities of building an addition to the main house, converting the basement to an ADU, or remodeling the entire house, but, ultimately, they decided that converting the existing Tuff Shed garage in the rear of the house would provide the best investment.

They brought Dyer in to design the ADU. The couple expressed that they wanted it to be a self-contained unit, which they imagined as a guest space or a short-term rental. This meant having a bedroom, a bathroom, a kitchen area with all necessary appliances, and a washer/dryer.

It was also important that the Tuff Shed garage door be replaced by sliding glass doors. The concern was that the ADU would be too dark in this shaded rear space, so having the large area of glazing would make it feel bright and comfortable.

Dyer says she approached the design of this space as if it were a cottage on the coast. It needed to be durable and functional, with simplicity of form. She wanted it to feel like a home away from home, made cozy with curated treasures and accents. Jodi says Dyer was brilliant in taking a 400-square-foot space and packing it with everything one would need to make it relaxing and homey.

A QUICK COMPLETION
AND THEN DELAYS

The conversion of the Tuff Shed garage to an ADU took just about five months. It then took another three months to get their short-term rental permit completed. By that time, the pandemic had shut down most travel and there were no vacationers needing a short-term rental. They were able to rent the ADU to a traveling nurse working in the local hospital, and, when she left, they listed the unit on Airbnb, and business picked up. One of the tenants liked the unit so much she asked to rent it on a long-term basis.

The owners say they were not really motivated to do this for the money or the investment, though it is a nice benefit. As an urban planner, Jodi says it is one of her core values to do what she can to make her city and community more vibrant and livable. So, her

Above: Double pocket doors between the living and bedroom areas create a flexible space to accommodate guests' preferences in the use of the space. Natural light permeates the unit through the sliding glass doors and windows on all sides. They are all placed to maintain privacy in the ADU while still bringing in lots of light.

Opposite: An opaque glass window in the bathroom allows in light to this small space but provides privacy.

Above left: The side yard patio, created out of the larger-than-standard setback, is perfect for outdoor meals and entertaining.

Above right: The open vaulted trussed ceiling, from the original garage, creates a light, connected space.

primary goal was to use their property to create additional density in a neighborhood that is zoned and designed to support more housing. Using the ADU as a short-term rental was a short-term solution for them to generate enough income to pay off their loan. But, eventually, they say, when their kids are grown and when Jeff and she are ready to downsize, they will consider moving back into this house so that they can return to a dense urban neighborhood where they can age in place.

While it was still being used for short-term rentals, Jodi and Jeff decided to use the ADU as a staycation themselves. They blocked out a night, went to dinner, and spent a night at the unit. Jodi says that after all the hard work getting it built, it was a great experience staying in such a cozy and welcoming place.

Jodi emphasizes that she could not have completed this project without the great knowledge, expertise, patience, and hard work of both her designer and general contractor.

TRUSS CEILINGS

Truss ceilings are structural frameworks of timbers designed to provide support for a roof or used to bridge the space above a room. The timbers appear at regular intervals and are linked by purlins or horizontal beams. These triangular structural parts tie the outside walls of the home together. Trusses are prefabricated wooden structures unlike rafters, which look like trusses but are usually built on-site. Trusses are designed to carry the necessary loads and the spacing requirements of the structure. Roof trusses are precision cut in a factory, so they are uniform throughout the structure. They are lightweight and faster and easier to install than some other framing systems. Because they have an open structure, it is easier to install electrical, plumbing, and heating and cooling systems in structures with trusses. They are available in many styles with a variety of pitches (slope) and spans (length). Some trusses are designed for second-floor living spaces in the attic. The trusses in this structure were originally part of the Tuff Shed garage, which was retrofitted to create this ADU. Designer Stephanie Dyer says, "The open vaulted ceiling makes the space feel airy and interconnected, with a playful nod to its origin as a truss-framed garage."

SOUTH SOUND ADU

SITE-BUILT

LOCATION: Olympia, Washington

PHOTOGRAPHER
Poppi Photography
www.poppiphoto.com

ARCHITECT
The Artisans Group
https://artisansgroup.com

GENERAL CONTRACTOR
JW Custom Construction

SIZE
400 square feet

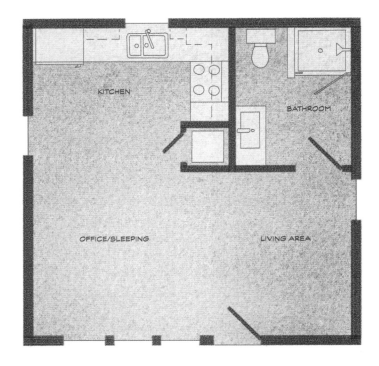

Sara and Peter Klinzman decided they wanted to build an ADU that could be used as Sara's therapy office, instead of paying rent for a separate location. Additionally, since they have a small house (1,000 square feet), they thought it would be nice to have guest space for family and friends. When Sara retires, the couple plans to rent out the ADU for short- or long-term use, while they begin to do more traveling themselves.

Below: The exterior of the house has fiber cement siding for easy maintenance and durability. The string lights around the house are LED garden lights and add a bit of whimsy to the exterior.

GREEN FEATURES

- All electric
- Low-flow faucets and showerhead
- Dual-flush toilet
- Car charging station
- Quartz countertops
- Fiber cement board

ENERGY FEATURES

- Ductless mini-split heat pump
- High efficiency insulation
- Concrete flooring
- High efficiency windows

Above: The closet next to the stove is currently used to store Sara's business records but it is plumbed for a washer/dryer, which the owners plan to install in the future.

When they decided to build their ADU, they approached Roussa Cassel, their neighbor, who is one of the architects and principles of The Artisans Group. She directed them to the company's four preapproved plans they designed for the City of Olympia Housing Authority. The couple selected the smallest of the plans, which was 480 square feet. Roussa reduced the space to 400 square feet for them to meet the demands of the site. Although a few of the walls were tweaked, the city allowed them to build the structure with no additional plans. People with eligible lots within the city limits have access to these free preapproved ADU plans.

PREAPPROVED PLANS

The couple decided the preapproved plans were a good option since they represented significant cost and time savings. According to Tessa Smith, a partner in The Artisans Group, "The individual using the preapproved plans doesn't have to pay architectural fees, which usually are around 10 percent of the cost of construction. In addition, the projects are already preapproved with the city so they don't have to go through a lengthy or expensive permitting process."

By working with a preapproved design through the city the homeowner is able to speed up the permitting process, typically from the standard three months to one month. For the Klinzmans, the building process took just about six months to complete.

FUTURE PLANS
FOR THE ADU

Since the ADU is currently being used as an office, there are minimal privacy concerns regarding the proximity of the main house to the ADU. When they decide to rent out the ADU in the future, the Klinzmans say they may consider putting in hardscape or foliage between the structures to create more privacy.

Sara is delighted they decided to build the ADU—they love the space and design. They only wish they had built it sooner and suggest "anyone thinking about building an ADU should do it."

Right: The bathroom has a frosted window for privacy. The toilet is dual flush and narrow to fit this small space. The flooring is polished concrete and the countertops are quartz.

Below: There are currently two oversized chairs in the living area. The owners plan to add a Murphy bed where the bookshelf now stands for use with family and other guests. The polished cement flooring provides a clean modern look and can serve as thermal mass, reducing the need for energy.

COMER ADU

SITE-BUILT

LOCATION: Avon, Connecticut

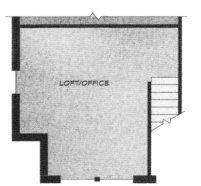

ARCHITECT/PHOTOGRAPHER
Jamie Wolf
Wolfworks Inc.
www.homesthatfit.com

CONSTRUCTION MANAGER
Janet Downey
Wolfworks Inc.

SIZE
1,316 square feet

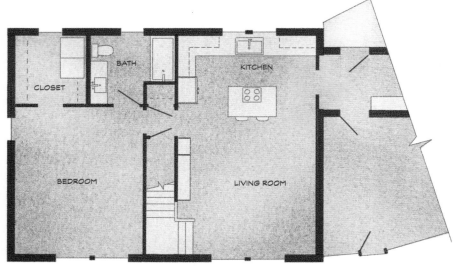

The Comers, Rob and Ali (with their young son), and his parents, Marty and Karin, wanted to build a home together, It needed to have separate living areas for each family—each space with materials and finishes in their preferred style, with the exterior providing coherence. Rob and Ali and their son would live in the main home, with Marty and Karin living in the ADU. Their intention from the start was to build a connected net-zero house, which was one of the reasons they called upon architect Jamie Wolf, a past winner of the Net Zero Challenge (Eversource) who has built several other net-zero homes.

Above: The ADU and main house are separated by the screen porch between them. It is both a buffer between the homes and a shared gathering space. Nestled behind the porch is the passage between the house and the ADU's separate mudroom entry, across from the garage. If the ADU residents ever need easy access, the walk from the garage to the ADU entry is continuous with no steps.

GREEN FEATURES

- Standing seam metal roof
- Heat recovery ventilator
- Cellulose insulation (see sidebar on page 111)

ENERGY FEATURES

- Triple-pane windows
- LED lights
- Heat pump water heater
- Heat pump heating and cooling
- ENERGY STAR appliances
- Airtight construction
- Ceiling fans
- Solar panels (on barn) and battery backup

DESIGNING THE HOUSE

The couples shared images of houses they liked with Wolf, some of which featured exposed beams. The house was then designed with timbers that are not structural but are meant to decoratively evoke the look of post and beam construction.

The couples wanted a modern gabled exterior in a dark finish. The ADU plan was to have a single large open kitchen, dining area, living area, and a bedroom suite. The addition of an upstairs loft room would be ideal for personal activities and the future option for live-in help or visiting guests. They wanted a large screen porch that both families could share. According to Wolf, everyone participated fully in the home design.

Above: Appliances in the kitchen are all full size; however, the oven was chosen for its accessibility and the door swings out rather than down. The microwave drawer was selected for the same reason.

Opposite: The entrance door has glass panels, which bring in additional light to the entry area. Just outside the front door is a covered landing with a seat (not seen in the photo).

LIVING A MULTIGENERATIONAL LIFE

Since three generations of family would be sharing this space, Wolf says it is significant that these aging parents and adult children liked each other (which is not always a given) and wanted to live close to each other. In addition, there is the reciprocal care advantage for all of them, with the grandparents assisting with childcare and the younger couple available for loving care as aging requires it. There is the option to spontaneously share a meal and visit when agreed upon. And since Marty and Karin travel for extended periods, with their shared arrangement, they don't need to worry about their home in their absence.

When designing a multigenerational house, Wolf says, it is important to know what the long-term use will be of the space, since the need is relatively short in relation to the life of the structure. In the case of this home, he says, the ADU is permitted to be rented, so that its future use is anticipated in the design. In some cases, the ADU could become the aging-in-place living area for the young generation as they become the elders and maybe even their kids can someday take their space. In other cases, the main house could be rented as an approach to financial retirement.

"The increase in interest in multigenerational living options is noticeable," says Wolf. He says he has built several and has new clients planning projects with aspects of shared living.

Left: The compact open floor plan looks large with its light-colored walls and two large windows, one on each side of the area.

Below: A large window in the bedroom brings in a good deal of light. Since they had a blue ceiling in their previous home, when they chose the bedroom ceiling color in the ADU, Marty held a color sample up to the blue sky and went with what he felt was a match.

Left: This second-floor loft space is used by Marty as his office and as an area where his young grandson can play.

Below: The porch between the house and ADU serves as a common area where both families can meet and relax.

CELLULOSE INSULATION

Cellulose insulation uses about 85 percent recycled paper and cardboard, which are two of the largest waste contributors to landfills. Boric acid is added to serve as a flame retardant and an insecticide. Cellulose can be sprayed into open wall cavities ("wall sprayed") or blown dry ("dense packed") into a closed wall behind either gypsum board or netting. In addition to reducing heat loss and air leaks, cellulose possesses a lower embodied energy, which means it takes less energy to produce this insulation than most other types of insulation products. Given the biogenic raw materials and their diversion from landfills, it is also one of the few (along with wood fiber insulation) carbon-storing insulations commercially available, lowering the carbon footprint of the house and helping the environment. Cellulose is also excellent at noise reduction—absorbing about 80 percent of the surrounding sound. The installed cost of cellulose is often higher than fiberglass batt insulation because the material itself is more expensive and installation a bit more expensive as well. It is a less expensive and more environmentally friendly option than any type of foam insulation. For more information, go to cellulose.org.

GREEN HOUSE ADU

SITE-BUILT

LOCATION: Minneapolis, Minnesota

PHOTOGRAPHER
Alyssa Lee Photography
www.alyssaleephotography.com

ARCHITECT
Christopher Strom Architects
https://christopherstrom.com

GENERAL CONTRACTOR
www.uberbuilt.com

SIZE
660 square feet

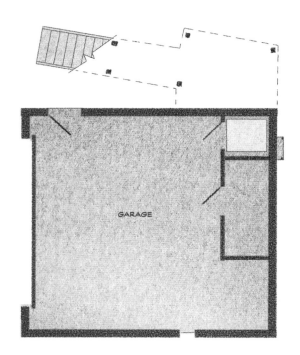

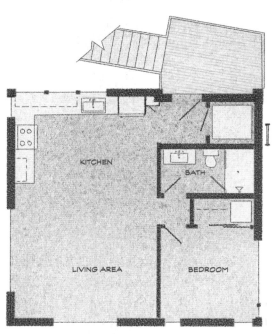

Opposite: The entrance is to the side of the structure. Solar panels can be seen on the roof.

After their garage burned down from an electrical short, homeowners Kirsten Jaglo and Michael Graven decided they would take the opportunity to build an ADU, which they had been considering for years. They say they were going to "make lemonade out of lemons, so to speak." Graven says the decision to build an ADU over the garage was more of a lifestyle decision than a financial one. They carefully selected materials and systems that they felt would be great choices for themselves and their family.

The ADU currently serves as a guest room, a yoga space, a place for holiday dinners, and for the couple's date nights. In the future, however, they plan for it to be a possible residence for extended aging family members. For that eventuality, they added an elevator to make it more universally accessible. In addition, they added other features to make it more comfortable and safe for family members to age in place.

INCORPORATING SOME UNIVERSAL DESIGN FEATURES

Including an elevator in the plan made the living area more accessible for anyone physically challenged. They also included a curbless shower (see sidebar on page 219), with grab bars and a seat. All the tile in the bathroom is high friction, to prevent slipping in the shower and in the surrounding area. On the shower trim, buttons were added to turn the water on and off without the need for levers that can be difficult for some people. All the handles on kitchen and bathroom cabinetry were designed for easy access. The toilet in the bathroom is wall-hung (see sidebar on page 167), which allows for about seven inches of extra floor space, compared to traditional toilets. Graven says the wall behind the toilet had to be about two inches thicker than usual to accommodate all the mechanicals, electrical and plumbing conduits—but it was a "game of inches," making the best use of the petite floor plan that they had to work with.

GREEN FEATURES
- Metal siding
- On-demand hot water
- Low VOC paint
- Induction stove
- Heat recovery ventilator

ENERGY FEATURES
- Solar panels
- Automated solar shades
- High efficiency insulation
- Mini-split heating/cooling
- In-floor radiant heating
- High efficiency windows
- LED Lighting

Right: Sparse, Danish-style furnishings were used. The couple chose a linoleum flooring (see sidebar on page 119) with some cork added, a bio-based product that is highly durable, nontoxic, antimicrobial, and easy to maintain. The walls have low VOC paint.

DESIGNING THE ADU

The couple decided to contact Christopher Strom Architects to design this project because of their vast experience with ADUs, and Strom's work as an advisor to the City of Minneapolis's zoning staff when the City Council approved an amended zoning code allowing ADUs. Since energy efficiency and sustainability were major priorities for them, they felt Strom's architecture firm had the eco-conscious professionals for the job.

Opposite: Lots of light comes into the kitchen through multiple windows and a skylight. Since Jaglo likes a lot of color, she chose blue custom cabinets for the lowers and a light tan for the uppers. The couple chose full-size appliances, except for the dishwasher, to make cooking easier.

Right: The barrier-free shower (see sidebar on page 219) along with the grab bars, seat, and high-friction tiles make this a safer environment for showering.

Below: The bedroom has multiple windows for natural light and ventilation. The mini-split unit can be seen on the wall.

ENERGY EFFICIENCY AND SUSTAINABILITY PRIORITIES

Jaglo and Michael opted for solar panels to provide energy to the ADU as well as offset the energy used in the main house. In order to include a skylight in the bathroom for natural light, they eliminated a few solar panels but still have enough to provide adequate energy for the ADU on sunny days. When the sun is down, the unit is attached to the grid for energy. The house and ADU are tied to the grid and benefit from net metering (see sidebar on page 202), which means the utility buys back excess energy produced by the solar panels and reimburses the homeowner. For their many windows, they installed automated roller shades to limit the solar gain in the summer and minimize solar loss in the colder months.

Although the couple's child is still young, they can foresee a time when they might be ready to downsize and live in the ADU, while renting out their home. The couple built the ADU that they feel they could comfortably live in themselves, as well as for their guests.

Left: The front door adds a pop of color with the bright blue. Decking for the entranceway is a composite material made from bamboo and recycled plastic.

NOT YOUR GRANDMA'S LINOLEUM

Linoleum has come a long way from the early twentieth century when it was mostly used for kitchen flooring and commercial spaces because it was water resistant, easy to maintain, and low cost. What it lacked in style, it made up in durability.

Linoleum was out of style for many years, with the popularity of other floorings such as vinyl and laminates, but it has made a comeback in recent years as people have become more concerned about the environment and are more careful about bringing toxic materials into their homes. Linoleum has had a renewed popularity and is now considered a very environmentally friendly alternative made from natural materials such as solidified linseed oil, pine resin, ground cork, wood dust, mineral fillers such as calcium carbonate, and natural pigments, which are all biodegradable and nontoxic. Linoleum does not emit VOCs (volatile organic compounds), and it is fully recyclable and antibacterial. Its surface repels dust and dirt, making it hypoallergenic. Linoleum is durable, low maintenance, water-resistant, and is also available in a wide variety of colors and patterns. The only negatives are that it requires professional installation and furniture can cause it to dent. Homeowner Graven says he chose linoleum because it is a healthier option, is softer underfoot, and there were a wide variety of pattern and color choices available from Forbo, the flooring manufacturer.

ART COLLECTORS' ADU

SITE-BUILT

LOCATION: San Francisco, California

PHOTOGRAPHER
Daniel Lunghi
www.lunghistudio.com

ARCHITECT
Matthew Peek
Studio Peek Ancona
www.peekancona.com

GENERAL CONTRACTOR
Teutonic Construction
www.teutonic-cm.com

SIZE
850 square feet

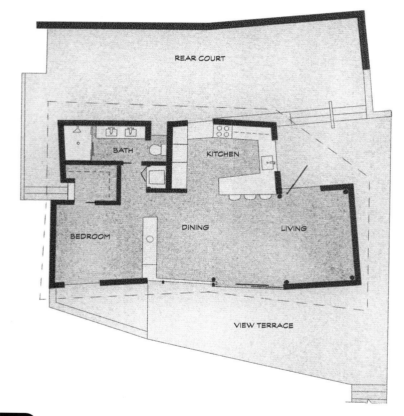

Bruce Johnston and Tom Noll (along with their Havanese, Pico) were living in an historic, mid-century house, designed by prominent architect William Wilson Wurster, until they decided to gift it to Bruce's daughter and son-in-law. Bruce says he wanted a different lifestyle, with no lawn-mowing or other maintenance projects. He says, "As I approached my eighties and could no longer wield garden tools or paintbrushes with skill, I imagined a much smaller house. We went from 3,000 square feet to 850, and my daughter and her spouse took over the original home and all its upkeep."

Below: Large roof overhangs limit solar gain during the warmer months when the sun is high in the sky and allow solar gain in the colder months when the sun is lower.

GREEN FEATURES

- Rain catchment system
- EPA-certified fireplace
- Earthquake-proof with steel columns
- No/low VOC finishes

ENERGY FEATURES

- LED lighting
- Radiant floor heating
- Super-insulated roof
- Large overhangs
- Concrete flooring
- Cross ventilation
- Tankless water heater
- ENERGY STAR water fixtures and appliances

Bruce and Tom realized that an ADU would be the most efficient means of building a new home for themselves close to their family. Economic efficiency was a requirement, particularly given the relatively steep hillside, limited access, and the earthquake fault below. The maximum allowable area for the ADU was 849 square feet, with a maximum height of fourteen feet. Bruce and Tom engaged architect Matthew Peek to design the structure after being impressed by his other work. The duo left most of the ADU design decisions to him.

DESIGN GOALS

The couple wanted a more modern, whimsical ADU than their main house, so they asked for "an architectural work of art that would house their large art collection." Because the house is located almost directly over a major fault line, the challenge was to build a high-strength home with an efficient construction schedule, budget, and operating cost.

Matthew designed the house to be resilient, eco-friendly, and make use of sustainable materials. He incorporated passive solar techniques, with a super-insulated roof, high-performance LED lighting, and radiant floor heating combined with a mini-split system and a small EPA-certified fireplace that would serve as a warm evening background to the living and dining areas. A rain catchment system would be used to irrigate the hillside below, limiting water consumption.

Opposite: The dining area sits close to the kitchen and the fireplace, which is more for atmosphere than heating. The couple says the fireplace functions mainly as a pedestal for their sculptures.

Below: The large kitchen includes ENERGY STAR appliances and a counter for casual meals.

NO WINDOW BLINDS REQUIRED

Matthew used a computer model to ensure that almost no direct light enters the space, except for some periodic light beams in the winter, which fall on limited floor areas to add warmth. This was mainly done to protect the artwork.

Given the very complex terrain, a tall, rear retaining wall, and tall trees, there are few privacy issues, and the house below is owned by Bruce's daughter. The adjacent properties have limited views to the sides of the building, which have only top clerestories, including in the bathroom—well above head height for privacy

Right: The multiple windows, sliding glass doors, and clerestory windows (see sidebar on page 129) bring natural light into the living area. Flooring is exposed concrete slab-on-grade, with radiant heat.

Left: Even the bathroom is filled with beautiful artwork from the owners' collection.

Opposite: Both paintings and sculptures adorn the bedroom area. The bedroom and bathroom areas don't require the more structural walls—that resist lateral forces, typically wind and seismic loads—used in other parts of the ADU. Windows and doors are situated to allow for cross-ventilation.

SEISMICALLY SENSITIVE CONSTRUCTION

To deal with the location of the ADU on the steep fault line, Matthew developed an innovative seismic system. This consists of twelve-foot-tall steel columns vertically embedded in a lightweight concrete foundation reinforced with an underground concrete grid. The columns are joined by lightweight special steel frames, whose assembly of beams and columns rigidly resist both vertical and lateral forces.

Since wall space for the couple's paintings was essential, the construction plan took that into consideration. The steel and concrete are strategically placed to reduce costs, resulting in a composite frame, with most of the materials in wood. The steel columns are inset from the exterior wood

walls. This allows for surround clerestory windows (see sidebar on page 129) atop the wood framing for natural lighting, and a view of the surrounding tree canopy. The multitude of paintings are mounted on the white-painted walls below the clerestory windows and are highlighted by the light above them. The excavation allowed for an eight-foot retaining wall on the uphill side of the ADU, poured with the ADU foundation slab, stabilizing the earth, and providing shade and earth cooling from the strong southern light.

This solution provided a stable structure while also allowing for panoramic mountain views north and enough wall space for the couple's art. With the stability of the steel column structure, they were able to eliminate interior structural walls and allow for an open floor plan.

AN INNOVATIVE WATER CATCHMENT SYSTEM

Instead of typical drainage, the roof is minimally pitched to one double drain with an integrated overflow device, facilitating water release during storms. This decreases the weight of pooling water on the roof and reduces debris from surrounding redwood trees from clogging the gutters. Water is collected for rain harvesting in a cistern that feeds the landscape during dry months and stabilizes the soil.

Above: An aerial shot shows the main house and the ADU on the hill behind it.

Opposite: Clerestory windows bring in ample light and highlight the many works of art in the ADU.

FUTURE PLANS

Bruce and Tom plan to build a 120-square-foot shed in the rear of their ADU to serve as a library. They say it will have the same type of clerestory windows as their ADU. Currently the couple uses energy from the main house's solar panels for their home and hybrid Volt car, and there is enough energy for both structures. In the future, Bruce and Tom plan to add solar panels and battery storage to their ADU to make the ADU more independent of the main house.

CLERESTORY WINDOWS

Clerestory windows are set at the top of a wall and allow daylight into a house or ADU with only a small amount of heat gain. Clerestory windows can be operable or fixed. If these windows open, they can also facilitate cross ventilation in a room where one or more walls might otherwise not have windows. In this house, south-facing clerestory windows let in the low sunlight for solar gain in the winter, while the overhangs provide shade from the higher sun in the summer. Clerestory windows are particularly practical for small houses and ADUs because they allow light and ventilation to enter the room without taking up needed wall space.

HAMILTON COURT ADU

SITE-BUILT

LOCATION: Los Altos, California

PHOTOGRAPHER
Slava Blazer Photography
www.slavablazer.com

ARCHITECT
Cottage
www.cotta.ge

GENERAL CONTRACTOR
Venture Construction & Development
www.venturecdi.com

SIZE
748 square feet

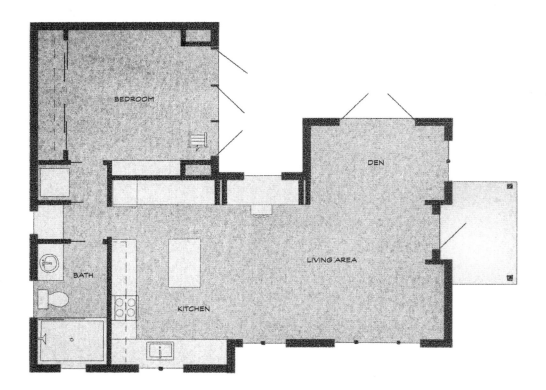

Leslie and Bob decided to build an ADU when their daughter Alison opted to move back home. Realizing they needed extra space, they decided an ADU would be a more cost-effective option than Alison needing to rent a nearby apartment. This would not only provide a home for their daughter, but also add equity to their property and possibly provide a place for them to live sometime in the future.

The L-shaped ADU was strategically placed at the corner of the lot, blocking a view of the neighbor's home, to create more privacy in their backyard. Leslie and Bob both have a passion for architecture, so both were involved in all aspects of the design and construction process, selecting many of the components.

Below: Exterior siding is fiber cement, which is highly durable and long lasting. Solar panels on the roof provide energy for the ADU as well as the main house.

GREEN FEATURES
- Induction stove
- Quartz countertops
- All electric
- Low-flow faucets, showerheads, and toilet

ENERGY FEATURES
- Solar panels
- Tankless water heater
- Mini-split heating/cooling
- Smart heat pump dryer

DESIGNING THE ADU

The couple had previous experience building one house and remodeling two others, doing disaster repair work as volunteers, and building houses in Mexico. They listened to seminars about ADUs online, and did a good deal of research through books, magazines, and the internet. Once they began the design process with Cottage, the couple stayed involved with weekly meetings. Since they lived just steps from the construction, they were able to inspect the progress daily and keep in touch with the construction superintendent.

Opposite: Two sets of double French doors lead out to the patio. Half of the patio has grout between the joints; the other half has decomposed granite in the joints for natural drainage. Custom cabinetry provides storage in every possible space, including here by the entrance.

Below: An open concept and vaulted ceilings create a more spacious feel than its square footage would appear to provide. The full kitchen includes all full-size appliances, including an induction stove. A desk nook and bookshelf in the kitchen area add character and convenient storage.

Leslie and Bob interviewed several architectural firms, but Cottage seemed to be the best fit for them. Because of Cottage's relationship with Venture Construction this was a design-build situation that they liked better than having to put the plans out to bid.

Their goals for the design of the ADU were to build with quality materials, high energy efficiency, and lots of light while maximizing the use of the limited space.

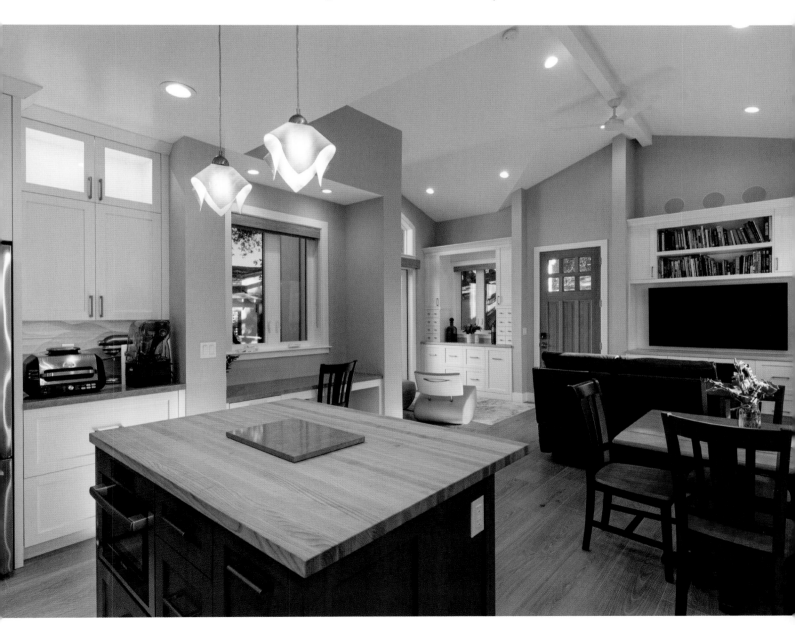

ENERGY EFFICIENCY AND LOW MAINTENANCE A PRIORITY

With energy savings a priority, the ADU was built with maximum insulation, an on-demand water heater, a ductless mini-split system, and high efficiency windows. Solar panels were installed that provide energy to the ADU and also the main house.

The couple's desire to keep the structure low maintenance guided them in the selection of appliances and materials. Porcelain tile that looks like oak wood planks was used for the flooring because it is waterproof, scratchproof, and won't have to be refinished. Quartz was used for the countertops for its durability. Porcelain backsplash tiles were installed up to the bottom of the cabinets, making it easy to keep clean. Landscaping was kept natural and low maintenance as well.

Construction of the ADU took twenty months due to Covid delays and supply chain issues. Alison was able to move into the ADU after living in her parents' spare bedroom during construction. When it was completed, it provided her more space, privacy, and storage. The couple say their daughter loves the ADU and they like having her close by.

Left: A small drop-leaf table provides a place to eat in addition to the island seating.

Top: The bedroom has ample storage with a black box system from the Container Store. The space above the flat ceilings of the kitchen, bath, and hallway is a storage loft which can be accessed with the library ladder in the bedroom. Barn doors above the closet provide access to additional storage. The 10-foot ceilings in the ADU provided extra space that the couple decided to use for storage, much needed in a small home. The stacked washer and heat pump dryer are just outside the bedroom.

Bottom: Bob says he likes the way the barrier-free shower looks but also prefers it because it is safer than more traditional showers. He considers the possibility he and Leslie might someday live in the ADU and this shower makes it possible for a walker or wheelchair to be used, if needed. Tiles on the floor and all walls go up to the ceiling, providing a very sustainable and clean option.

HEAT PUMP DRYERS

Heat pump dryers heat the air, using it to remove moisture from the clothes and then reusing it once the moisture is removed. Unlike a conventional dryer which releases warm, humid air through a dryer vent to the exterior of the house, a heat pump dryer sends the air through an evaporator to remove the moisture without losing much heat. A refrigerant is used as part of this process, and less electricity is used to generate heat. The moisture removed from the air with the evaporator, during the drying process, results in water that needs to be drained. Water can be manually drained from the tank with a hose that discharges the water into a nearby sink or drainpipe.

There are several advantages to using heat pump dryers, particularly in small homes and ADUs. Since they don't require a vent to the outside, there are fewer openings in the exterior envelope. Compact models can be installed in small spaces and stacked with a washing machine as they were in this house. They can be placed in any area of the house where there is access to water and electricity. They are also easier to install because they don't require outdoor ventilation and they reduce the energy generally used to dry clothes by about 28 percent compared to standard dryers. Because clothes are dried at a lower temperature, heat pump dryers are also gentler on clothes. ENERGY STAR certified dryers have moisture sensors that can save time and energy and prevent clothes from over-drying. Some models have anti-wrinkle technology, smart settings, and remote smartphone controls.

LANGFORD AVENUE LANEWAY

SITE-BUILT

LOCATION: Toronto, Canada

PHOTOGRAPHER
Robert Burley
https://robertburley.com

ARCHITECT
LGA Architectural Partners
https://lga-ap.com

GENERAL CONTRACTOR
Vanderwal Builds
www.vanderwalbuilds.ca

SIZE
1,184 square feet

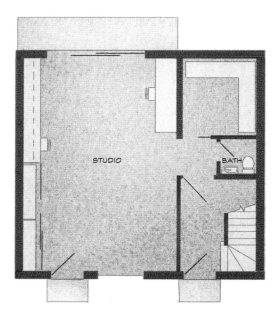

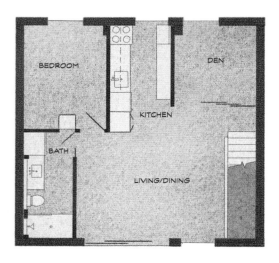

Opposite: The remaining rear garden was transformed into a landscaped courtyard between the laneway and the main house.

After Debra Friedman and Robert Burley's three sons moved out of the family home, the couple decided to build a laneway on their former parking pad and a small part of their garden. Bob Burley is an architectural photographer and a recently retired professor from Toronto Metropolitan University; Debra Friedman is a portrait photographer. The laneway currently serves as an at-home studio for both, as well as a source of income to cover the cost of its construction. In the future they will have the flexibility to downsize and age in place in the laneway and rent out their house to maintain income and supplement the rising value of their property.

GREEN FEATURES
- Energy recovery ventilator
- Engineered hardwood

ENERGY FEATURES
- Hydronic radiant in-floor heating
- On-demand water heater
- Ceiling fans

REQUIREMENTS FOR THE LANEWAY

Architects at LGA Architectural Partners are long-time friends who also worked on the couple's main house renovation in 2014. At that time, Debra and Bob had the firm design a garage/studio for their backyard, which they didn't end up building. By the time they were ready to rethink the plan, the City of Toronto had passed new bylaws allowing for the construction of laneway suites. The couple knew LGA Architectural Partners could execute "a smart, practical design" that could be achieved within their budget. Although this was a small building project, Bob and Debra understood from the outset that it was a complicated job that had to be executed with great attention to detail since laneways were still a new concept. Robert says, "Many of the problems that needed to be solved were as new as the laneway house bylaws and they needed an architect that could learn on the go." With LGA's great design skills, previous experience with the complexities of ADUs, and a full team of support professionals, Robert knew they were the group for the project.

ENERGY EFFICIENCY AS A PRIORITY

The couple felt energy efficiency was very important in the design. As a rental unit, it was particularly important to have an easy-to-use design that also balanced passive approaches with more active systems to achieve a comfortable, well-sealed, well-ventilated space. The design of the HVAC system is both compact and efficient and suited to a small urban site. Fresh air is provided throughout both floors using an energy recovery ventilator (ERV), and the contractor installed shorter duct runs to maximize the ceiling heights while also decreasing the amount of energy required to push air throughout. Hydronic radiant in-floor heating is assisted by integrated baseboard heaters. The water in the radiant flooring is heated by a high-efficiency, gas-fired, on-demand water heater which supplies domestic hot water as well.

Operable window placement provides cross ventilation on both floors and ensures daylight harvesting deep within the rooms, including a light tunnel in the second-floor washroom. Efficient, high-quality wall unit air-conditioners were provided on each floor for very hot days and are augmented with ceiling fans to help move the cool air throughout the rooms.

Opposite: The upstairs residential suite consists of a living-dining room, a bedroom, bathroom, kitchen, and a den. Blue highlights tie the different spaces together.

Below: On the ground floor is the studio where both Debra and Robert run their business. There are two workstations in the office area, and everything is mobile, including tables, chairs, and equipment. According to Robert, sometimes it's an office, and at other times a photo studio. It also frequently becomes a print/framing studio and every now and then they transform it into a social space for parties and dinners. Flooring on the ground floor is concrete with an epoxy finish.

LOW MAINTENANCE REQUIRED

Durability was important, and the choice of materials on the exterior, in the studio, and in the rental suite were each carefully considered. All exterior materials—both the standing seam and the shou sugi ban planks (see sidebar on page 144)—have long lifespans with little or no maintenance. In addition, a generous canopy above the wood protects it from the elements. The exterior walls were designed as a rain screen so that any moisture that did get in drained freely away from the building. Since the studio is a workspace and an extension of the outdoors during temperate months, it was important that the floors were easy to clean and could withstand high traffic with tall baseboards to protect the walls. The mechanical systems are simple and easy to operate with long life spans and will also be easy to update in the future.

Above left: Wall-to-roof windows in the rooms facing the main house ensure both daylight and privacy.

Above right: The bathroom is luxurious with a wall-hung toilet (see sidebar on page 167), fully tiled walls, and a towel warmer.

ENGINEERED FLOORING

Engineered wood is an environmentally friendly alternative to solid-wood flooring that creates less waste and requires cutting down fewer trees. With a core made of layers of strengthened composite plywood or oriented strand board (OSB), covered with a choice of wood veneers, the flooring is very durable and minimizes expansion and shrinkage due to temperature and humidity changes. Since it is not as vulnerable to the effects of the variability of moisture and temperature as solid hardwood and is less likely to warp, engineered flooring can even be installed in kitchens and bathrooms.

Engineered floors are easier to install than solid hard woods and are versatile in the ways they can be installed and used. They can be nailed, glued down, or installed as floating (which means they're connected to each other but not fastened to the floor). They can be installed below, on, or above grade (solid wood can't be installed below grade). Engineered flooring comes in a wide variety of species, grades, thickness, widths, and finishes and, as an added advantage, engineered flooring usually costs less than solid hardwood flooring.

SHOU SUGI BAN

Shou sugi ban (which translates to burnt cedar board) is a traditional Japanese technique of charring the outer surface of wooden cladding to make it rot and insect resistant. While the exact origins of shou sugi ban are unknown, it is estimated to have been in use in Japan since the 1700s. Several woods can be treated this way, including cedar, Douglas fir, and larch.

One of the original processes for producing shou sugi ban is done by binding boards together in a triangular tube and then burning the wood from the inside just deep enough to get a black-silver finish. In modern production settings the boards are charred using semi-automated machines that give the boards a consistent and even surface look and texture. The wood is sometimes left in a natural charred state, often referred to as "deep char," or the surface layer is wire brushed to remove some of the charring and then finished with oil or sealants to bring out the gray, silver, or other tones and deep grain textures.

This charring process preserves the wood, and makes it resistant to fire, rot, and pests. It is considered environmentally friendly because the wood does not need to be treated with any chemical preservatives and can be paired with an all-natural finish to maintain its appearance long term. Wood treated with this method can be used for exterior siding as well as interior furniture and paneling on walls. For further information, visit www.shousugiban.com.

FUTURE PLANS
FOR THE LANEWAY

Robert says they expect the living quarters to offer them increased flexibility in the future. Before starting the laneway unit they renovated their basement with underpinning and new living space. In the future, they expect that their property could easily accommodate three families by duplexing the main house and keeping the living area/workspace in the laneway unit. They may even end up living in the laneway living quarters in the future. With three sons, their main house and laneway unit could easily be transformed into a multigenerational compound.

Below: The yellow door is the entrance to the residence and the blue door goes into the studio.

CEDAR COTTAGE ADU

SITE-BUILT

LOCATION: Seattle, Washington

PHOTOGRAPHER
Cindy Apple Photography
www.cindyapple.com

ARCHITECT
Stefan Hampden (principal architect)
Adam Clements (project architect)
CAST architecture
www.castarchitecture.com

GENERAL CONTRACTOR
Scott Construction

SIZE
467 square feet

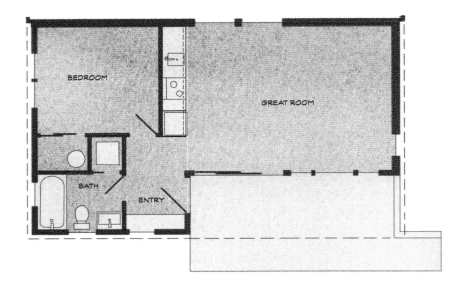

C had and Dana Phelan decided to build an ADU in their back-yard to have space for guests while their kids are young, and the option to move into the ADU when their kids are grown. It also has been a source of additional income; they use it for short-term rentals when they don't have friends or family staying with them.

The couple did a web search to find architects with good experience designing ADUs and they chose CAST architects after seeing their vast portfolio. After the ADU was completed, the couple allowed the architects to offer the design to the City of Seattle to use as a preapproved plan for other homeowners.

The design of the DADU includes sixty-four square feet of covered outdoor living space. The generous overhang allows it to be used in all weather, and with good lighting it can be used in the evenings as well. The entrance door is frosted to bring in light but still provide privacy.

The exterior of the house is clad in cedar which is a locally sourced, sustainable material. The sloped roof allows for high ceilings and lots of light to come into the house. Windows were carefully placed; several of the windows are frosted and some are clerestory, allowing ventilation and light while providing privacy. The large frontal windows and porch expand the living space and give the ADU the feel of being larger than it is. The orientation and siting among large evergreen trees help ensure privacy.

GREEN FEATURES
- Recycled and renewable materials

ENERGY FEATURES
- Concrete floors
- LED lighting
- Large overhang
- Mini-split heating/cooling
- Solar ready roof

Above: A small area near the entranceway is the perfect place to store coats, wet boots, and shoes.

Opposite: The living room is oriented toward the bank of glazing, bringing in an abundance of natural light. Glass doors extend the living space outdoors and provide beautiful views. The extended Baltic birch plywood ceiling brings extra warmth to this cozy ADU. Flooring throughout the ADU is stained concrete.

SITE APPROPRIATE AND PRIVACY

One of the couple's main concerns was building the ADU to be sensitive to the site conditions. They wanted to be careful to preserve the two large mature trees and their roots on the property. The house was therefore built with a shallow foundation that would not disrupt the roots and allow the tree enough room to flourish. Another concern was the very tall house next door to the property. Taking this into consideration, Stefan Hampden, a principal at CAST architecture, designed the house with a shed roof that slants away from the neighbor. That side of the house has minimal windows, thus securing privacy.

Since the ADU will be used by renters, Chad and Dana also wanted to assure privacy between the two structures on the property. Therefore, most of the windows are on one side of the house, away from the main house and adjoining property, which provides the most privacy and brings in a good deal of light.

EXPANDING THE LIVING SPACE

The ADU was designed with a large, covered patio, which makes the house feel more expansive than its size would suggest. The large window wall opens to the living space and makes it feel like a large open area. The concrete foundation was used for the interior flooring and concrete pavers were used for the patio, which makes the patio feel like an extension of the house. Building the ADU with the concrete flooring saved money on construction but also serves as thermal mass to help regulate the temperature inside the structure.

According to architect Hampden, "ADUs like the Cedar Cottage offer homeowners a degree of flexibility that traditional zoning has not been able to accommodate. These structures are small by nature but can have an outsized impact on the lives of the clients by giving them flexibility, and on communities in which they are built by providing more affordable, sustainable, and diverse housing."

The Cedar Cottage ADU was named the 2022 AIA Seattle Home of Distinction.

Opposite: The kitchen is open to the living room as part of the efficient floor plan. Daylighting is optimized and windows are thoughtfully placed for privacy.

Above left: The bedroom is at the back of the ADU and includes full-height storage and a washer/dryer in the closet.

Above right: The small bathroom has cheery aqua walls and two clerestory windows as well as two smoked lower windows for privacy and natural ventilation.

MARION AVENUE ADU

SITE-BUILT

LOCATION: Palo Alto, California

PHOTOGRAPHER
Alex Jopek
www.aejopek.com

ARCHITECT
Cottage
www.cotta.ge

GENERAL CONTRACTOR
Venture Construction & Development
www.venturecdi.com

SIZE
227 square feet

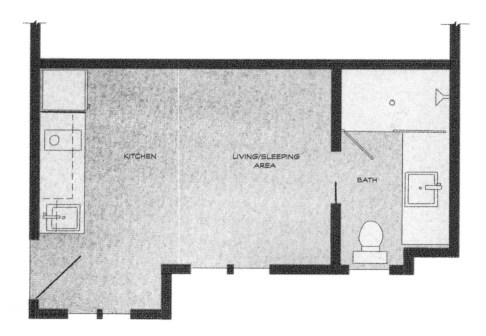

Christine and Stanley decided to add an ADU to their current home since Stanley was approaching retirement and they were looking to bring in extra income. The couple knew this would be a good, reliable source of retirement income. In their area there are many single people working in the local tech companies, as well as those attending Stanford University's graduate and professional schools, who are looking for places to live. They knew that there was a demand for this type of housing.

GREEN FEATURES

- All electric
- Induction cooktop
- Quartz tile
- Engineered wood flooring
- Dual-flush toilet

ENERGY FEATURES

- High efficiency insulation
- Mini-split heating/cooling
- ENERGY STAR appliances
- LED lights
- Halogen oven/microwave, requiring less energy usage than a conventional oven

ADDING AN ADDITION TO THEIR HOME

The homeowners wanted to ensure that their new ADU matched the look and feel of the existing home and blended in with the surrounding neighborhood.

Tying in the new ADU directly with the existing garage roofline, matching the stucco and roofing tiles perfectly, using the same window manufacturer and window style, and constructing a second matching dormer made the attached unit blend in perfectly with the main home. By extending the former garage for the attached ADU, the homeowners were able to fit this additional unit into a surprisingly efficient footprint on their primary residence.

Neighbors who see the new addition to their home are often surprised at how well the ADU ties into the architecture and construction of the main house and find it difficult to remember this house before the outdoor covered driveway space was converted. In addition to the added income from the ADU, the owners feel the new addition adds curb appeal to their main home. The ADU also adds additional value to their property, converting an unused carport into interior finished space. The extra square footage is valued at the same price per square foot as their main house, so it improves their property value and their equity in it.

The ADU was added nineteen years after the couple bought their house. In prior years, they were not able to add an ADU, as their lot was too small under the zoning laws to qualify at that time. Several new laws have since been passed in the state of California, allowing ADUs to be built to help alleviate California's severe housing shortage.

SELECTING COTTAGE TO BUILD THEIR ADU

Opposite: This is the original house before the ADU was added.

Below: Although the kitchen is small it has all the necessary appliances with a combination microwave/halogen oven/vent hood/range light, additional under-cabinet LED lighting, quartz countertops, full tile backsplash, a 2-burner induction cooktop, a counter-depth refrigerator, and extra tall custom cabinets for additional storage.

Christine contacted several companies that build ADUs. Many of them only wanted to build stand-alone units, and some wanted to alter the current garage along with building the ADU. Others would only design a modern ADU, which would not go along with her more traditional home. She says Cottage had excellent architects to design the unit, a fully licensed and bonded contractor to build it, and they do all the legwork getting the permits and working with the city building department. Christine was pleased with the price and the company's willingness to work with the style the couple wanted,. The result exceeded their expectations.

QUALITY OVER QUANTITY

With just 227 square feet to work with, Cottage's architects and contractor designed the attached small home to feel significantly roomier than expected. The owners carefully selected interior finishes and other details for quality and durability. They wanted this small space to have all the amenities of a larger dwelling, as well as high quality components. In addition to a full kitchen, the unit has a combination washer/dryer and a highly efficient heating and cooling system. Quality materials such as engineered white oak hardwood flooring, a custom tile-in shower, and a custom quartz bathroom vanity counter were incorporated. Several of the energy-efficient appliances are also WI-Fi enabled, such as the combo washer/dryer, the mini-split system, and the refrigerator.

They added on several other amenities such as a smart smoke detector and carbon monoxide monitor and an app-enabled front door light, which can be switched on by the tenant's phone before arriving home at night.

Left: The 16-foot vaulted ceilings and large windows let ample light into the space. The bathroom has a pocket door, saving space and improving the flow of the unit. Heating and air-conditioning are handled separately by a mini-split unit seen on the wall.

AN OCCUPIED SPACE

Just a few weeks after it was listed on the market, the unit was quickly rented to a tenant who works in one of the large flagship local technology firms. When the new tenant moved into the unit, the ADU was immediately furnished with items that would make the best use of the space. A pull-out trundle bed/daybed makes the bedroom double as a living space, a spacious mirrored wardrobe (not seen) expands the visual size of the space, and a combination desk/dining table and a mirrored entryway cabinet take advantage of every inch of the small floor space.

The owners are delighted with the ADU and credit the excellent contractors who worked around supply chain shortages, and expended thoughtful planning, to complete the unit and pass their final inspection in less than a year.

Above: A two-burner induction stovetop is functional and space saving.

Left: The bathroom design is a particular favorite of Christine's, because Cottage's architects made it feel like a spa. The full bathroom includes a washer/dryer, custom tile-in shower, porcelain sink, large lighted mirror, and custom quartz bathroom vanity counter.

SMALL APPLIANCES

With the increase in ADUs, small houses, tiny houses, and small apartments, kitchens are also usually smaller and require smaller appliances. Today many appliance manufacturers are meeting this need by producing beautiful, high-performance, small-space appliances—freestanding and built-in. According to the Association of Home Appliance Manufacturers, generational shifts, a desire to downsize, and interest in the small-home concept has driven an increase in the compact appliance market.

Some companies have discovered that eco-conscious millennials are interested in small-space appliances because they use less energy to run compared to full-sized units.

These small-space appliances are available in sizes from eighteen to twenty-eight inches wide in refrigerators, ranges, exhaust hoods, dishwashers, built-in coffee makers, and washers and dryers.

The small-space appliance industry used to design products with only size in mind, leaving the appliances to appear dull and boring. Now manufacturers use a variety of colors and high quality materials—including stainless steel—and provide many features found in full-sized appliances, just on a smaller scale. Smaller cooktops are available in gas, electric, and induction.

Countertop space comes at a premium, so multifunctional appliances can be a great space saver in small units. This can be seen in the washer/dryer combo unit and the microwave/halogen oven that allows it to bake like a regular oven/externally vented cooktop exhaust fan in the Marion Avenue ADU. Because it's important that appliances don't protrude into open space, manufacturers are designing built-in models that sit flush with kitchen cabinetry. An advantage to induction cooktops is they do not get hot and can be used as extra counter space. Many luxury features are now available for small-space appliances with such items as custom panels to match their surrounding cabinetry, and a smart home app to alert the homeowner if the freezer door is accidentally left open.

In certain spaces, small-space appliances can make the kitchen appear more spacious and proportional than a full-sized appliance would. They also leave more room for storage, countertop surfaces, and dining areas. Today the design and performance of appliances are not compromised by size.

SILVER LAKE ADU

PANELIZED

LOCATION: Silver Lake, Los Angeles, California

PHOTOGRAPHER
Emi Kitawaki
www.byemirose.com

ARCHITECT/ MANUFACTURER/BUILDER
Cover Technologies, Inc.
www.buildcover.com

SIZE
450 square feet

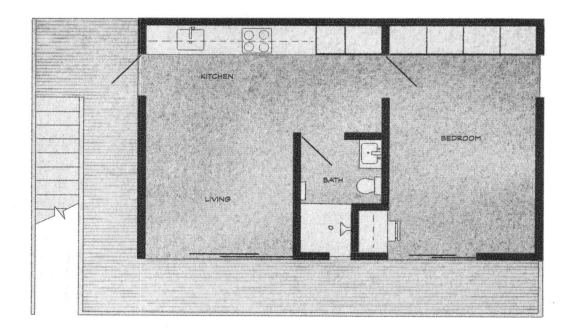

Opposite: The ADU sits atop a two-car garage, a wonderful amenity for guests.

Homeowners Michael Urban and Dean Anes bought their 1947-built home in 2012. There was a large section of land at the bottom of the property that they knew they could develop. Their dog enjoyed the open space, but the land wasn't otherwise being used, and keeping it maintained was more work than they wanted. They decided that building an ADU on this area of the property would be a way to generate some income, and it could eventually serve as a guesthouse.

GREEN FEATURES
- Thermally treated siding and deck
- All electric appliances
- Bamboo shelving
- Rainwater irrigation
- Energy-efficient rainscreen facade
- Induction stove
- Reduced waste with panelized
  system

ENERGY FEATURES
- Day lighting
- High efficiency windows and doors
- White reflective roof
- LED lights
- Mini-split heating/cooling
- Electronic shades

After their ADU was finished, their builder, Cover Technologies, rented the ADU as a model for the company. When that arrangement ends, the couple plans to use it for short-term rentals. Since they live in a trendy neighborhood, many people come to the area for the local art fairs or for television and film-related projects and are looking for an experience to live like a local.

A STREET-TO-STREET LOT

Their lot is "street to street" or a through lot, meaning the two ends of the lot have access to different streets. The ADU on the lot could have its own address and entrance; no one has to go by the main yard or house to get to the ADU. This creates a wonderful opportunity for access, separation, and privacy between the primary home and the ADU, one of the couple's priorities. They also oriented the views of the ADU toward the nearby hills. The resulting design has no windows toward the main home, with floor-to-ceiling windows on the side with the views.

Opposite: A concrete staircase leads from the garage to the ADU.

Below: The kitchen includes an induction cooktop, refrigerator, exhaust fan, and sink. The area opens to the living room/dining area and to the entrance hallway, lined with storage cabinetry.

BUILDING WITH A PANELIZED SYSTEM

When Michael and Dean were considering building an ADU, they initially thought it would be prohibitively expensive. After they read an article about Cover, it seemed like an easy way to build on the property without going over budget. Michael liked Cover's design aesthetic and the fact that they could provide blueprints and architectural renderings for a nominal cost. After the company gave them a tour of one of their existing properties, the couple decided there didn't seem to be a downside to building the ADU.

After extensive site work that went on during the pandemic lockdown, Cover took about a month to connect the panels together, assembling them like a Legos set.

In what used to be a natural hillside garden backyard, Cover built a retaining wall, a garage, and the ADU, completed in 2021.The modern ADU is a dramatic contrast to the primary Los Angeles home.

Left: Although the living space is compact, it is bright and airy with a wall of sliding doors and an exterior sitting area, extending the space. Flooring throughout the ADU is engineered white oak, attractive and indestructible.

Above: This barrier-free shower provides a clean, minimal appearance in this small space. The actual floor of the shower is the same material as the walls, with a drain in the center. The wood placed over the floor gives the shower more color and makes it slip-proof. The opaque window in the shower brings in light while also offering privacy.

Opposite: The bathroom sits behind the living room—both opening to the central hall. The bathroom has a wall-hung toilet (see sidebar on page 167) that provides more space than a traditional toilet. The windows and doors throughout the house are produced in-house by Cover in their factory in Gardena, Los Angeles.

WALL-HUNG TOILETS

A wall-hung toilet is particularly practical in ADUs and small houses, where every inch of space is essential. With its tank hidden away inside the wall, a wall-hung toilet adds up to twelve inches of floor space, depending on the toilet chosen. It uses about 20 percent less water than a standard toilet and is more hygienic because it doesn't rest on the floor,it is easier to clean beneath.

The concept was first introduced in Europe in the 1980s, but its popularity in the United States has vastly increased, particularly because of the current emphasis on smaller spaces, sustainability, and the increased interest in modern design. The three parts of the toilet are the tank (or in-wall carrier), the bowl/seat, and the flush panel, which comes in many styles. Some companies provide all the parts, and some require purchasing the tank from another supplier.

Mounting a wall-hung toilet is easier in new construction before drywall goes up; retrofitting requires that the wall and the floor be opened to accommodate the in-wall tank and drain. The tank can be installed in walls built with 2 by 4 or 2 by 6 studs. If the interior components need to be repaired or replaced, they can easily be accessed through the actuator plate.

Many of these units come with special features such as water-saving aspects, ADA compliancy, personal cleansing, an LED nightlight, and hands-free opening, closing, and flushing. Homeowners usually opt for wall-hung toilets because of their size and their clean, modern appearance.

FUTURE PLANS FOR THE ADU

Michael and Dean have older parents, and the couple can foresee a time one of them might move into the ADU. They also look forward to the 2028 summer Olympics in Los Angeles, which will be a great opportunity to rent out the space. Farther down the line, they might move into the ADU themselves because of the ease of having everything on one level. Renting out their main house, which has three bedrooms, would then become a source of revenue. Michael says, "Having an ADU on property, particularly in a city like Los Angeles, is the perfect solution to many problems, from the lack of affordable housing to the high price of retirement."

Above: The bedroom opens to the deck, offering natural light and ventilation.

Opposite top: A small desk in the bedroom accommodates those who might work remotely.

Opposite bottom: There is an abundance of storage throughout the ADU, including in the bedroom.

ADU PLUS

SITE-BUILT

LOCATION: Santa Monica, California

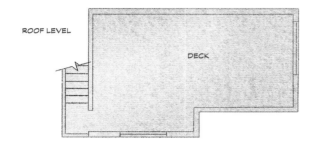

ROOF LEVEL

DECK

PHOTOGRAPHER
Art Gray
https://artgrayphoto.com

ARCHITECT/BUILDER
Patrick Tighe, FAIA
Tighe Architecture
www.tighearchitecture.com

SIZE
ADU 1,200 square feet
Studio apartment 420 square feet

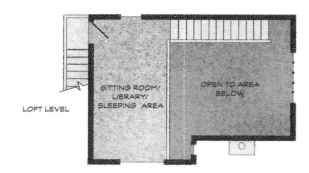

LOFT LEVEL

SITTING ROOM/ LIBRARY/ SLEEPING AREA

OPEN TO AREA BELOW

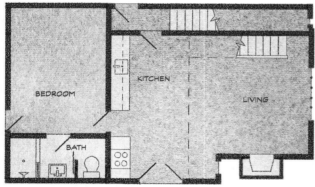

GROUND LEVEL

BEDROOM

KITCHEN

LIVING

BATH

Architect Patrick Tighe bought a 1950s home in Santa Monica that had originally been built to house Douglas Aircraft factory workers after World War II. The typical homes in the neighborhood were 1,400 square feet on a 5,000 square-foot lot. Many of the homes have since been replaced by much larger houses, which Tighe says has dramatically changed the character and scale of the neighborhood.

Instead of demolishing the house and building a much bigger one, Tighe chose instead to build an accessory dwelling unit as an addition to the original house. This was an alternative means of expanding his home, at a more affordable cost. The new attached residential dwelling added 1,200 square feet of living space to the existing 1,400 square-foot home. Tighe also built a studio apartment, which is located at a semi-subterranean level of the structure.

Tighe, the owner and architect, says, "Having come from the East Coast, we had always wanted to live in a loft-like space. The ADU was an opportunity to create our own loft here in Santa Monica, just a few blocks from the beach."

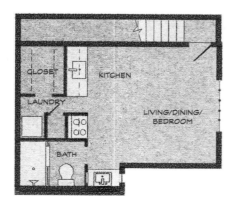

SUBTERRANEAN LEVEL

CLOSET

KITCHEN

LAUNDRY

LIVING/DINING/ BEDROOM

BATH

GREEN FEATURES

- Reclaimed, refurbished windows
- Cork flooring on the mezzanine level
- Vintage light fixture
- Quartz countertops

ENERGY FEATURES

- Mini-split heating/cooling
- Concrete floors

Preceding overleaf: The exterior of the ADU is wrapped in Corten steel siding. A green wall runs the length of the structure, and wisteria and trumpet vine intermix so that there is an abundance of flowers throughout the summer months. The plants climb the building and the flowers surround the roof deck on all sides.

Above left: The owners searched diligently for a prefabricated fireplace that had the best proportions and the largest opening. Tighe designed and fabricated a custom steel surround for a minimal presence in the room. The fireplace serves as a secondary source of heat.

Above right: The kitchen has a cooktop, sink, under-counter refrigerators, and quartz countertops.

Opposite: A high timber ceiling makes the room feel quite large and airy. Massive industrial refurbished windows, from a demolished mill in Detroit, bring in natural light and ventilation. The windows arrived, frames only, rusted and bent. Tighe revived the frames, painted them black, and added glass. The large aluminum globe is a vintage 1970s Italian light.

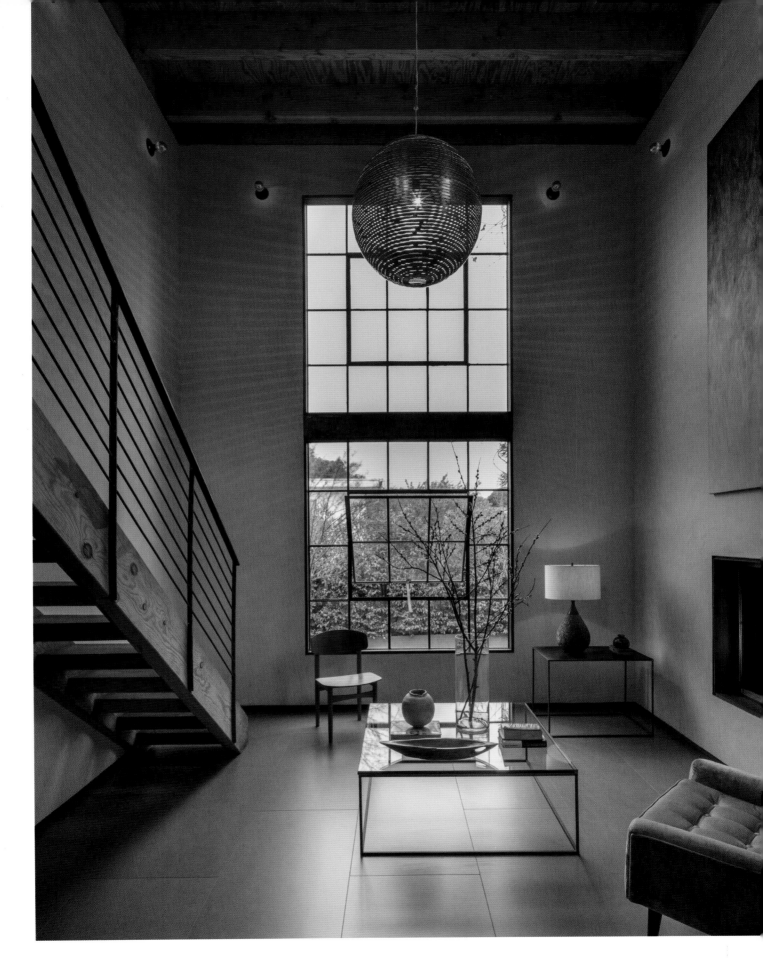

SUSTAINABLE AND FLEXIBLE

Exposed heavy timber construction defines the architecture in this ADU. The exterior volume is wrapped in Corten steel siding (sometimes known as weathered steel). Corten was developed by the military, and the metal was designed to rust on the surface and then stop oxidizing. The siding has a dark burnt red, almost brown, patina that is made to hold up well, even with its proximity to the ocean. Corten steel eliminates the need for painting, and if left outside exposed to the elements, it will develop a rusted appearance in just a few months.

The outside landscaping provides additional layers of texture, color, and ever-changing "life." The open plan of the new addition consists of the main living area with living room, kitchen and dining area, and a sleeping/sitting loft in the double-height floor above. There is also a separate suite in the lower level.

Left: The mezzanine level with cork flooring (see sidebar on page 177) is used as a sitting room, library, and sleeping area and is open to the living room. Flooring in the main level is two-by-four-foot porcelain tile over concrete.

Below left: Steel doors were custom made to be compatible with the reclaimed windows. The large door opens from the kitchen to an outdoor patio area.

Below right: The entrance pergola is covered with wisteria that grows and expands over time. An integrated trellis of heavy timber is attached to the building and serves as armature for more flora and defines the outdoor deck, with its outdoor barbecue.

A SIMPLE HEATING/COOLING SYSTEM

The house is heated and cooled with several mini-split units, along with a fireplace that is used for cooler days. The floors in the lower level are exposed concrete and, with its thermal mass, help cool the unit in the hotter months. Concrete tiles were used on the main level, which also benefits from its thermal mass quality.

Above: On the semi-subterranean level is a self-contained studio with a full kitchen, bathroom, laundry, and large walk-in closet. It has its own separate entry but is also accessible from the main house. The floors in the basement are exposed concrete that function as thermal mass, which allows for the building to be cool in the summer and retain heat in the colder winter months.

MULTIPLE USES FOR THE ADU/SUITE

The extra space was designed to be used by the owner's family, extended family, and for the many visitors that they have from the East Coast. Someday Tighe says he will downsize, and he may rent out one or more of the units. He designed the unit with optimal flexibility as the family unit expands and contracts. Currently an extended family member resides in the lower unit.

This project won an AIA LA Residential Award in 2020.

CORK FLOORING

Cork is considered an environmentally friendly material because it comes from the outer bark of cork oak trees that can be harvested every nine to fourteen years without harming the trees. Cork is ground up and coated with a nontoxic resin binder. Tiles, sheets, and tongue-and-groove strip flooring are available in a variety of colors, patterns, and thicknesses—the thicker tile is used for flooring because it is more shock and acoustic absorbent. There are lots of advantages to using cork flooring—it's natural, durable, easy to maintain, comfortable under foot, easy to install, hypoallergenic, does not absorb odors, and is resistant to moisture, mold, and mildew. The only downside is the need to refinish cork about every eight years.

SEVENS ADU

STRUCTURAL INSULATED PANELS (SIPS)

LOCATION: San Jose, California

PHOTOGRAPHER
Jean Bai
www.jeanbai.com

ARCHITECT
Adam Mayberry, AIA
Mayberry Workshop
www.mayerryworkshop.com

GENERAL CONTRACTOR
Merkouris Construction Inc.
www.merkourisconstructioninc.com
Green Galaxy Builders, Inc. (SIPs)
www.greengalaxybuilders.com

MANUFACTURER
Premier SIPS
www.premierbuildingsystems.com

SIZE
900 square feet

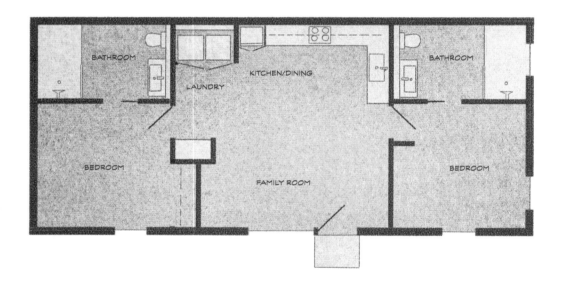

Gayle and David Barry decided to build an ADU to generate extra income, create a space that could potentially house aging parents, and eventually provide them with comfortable housing to age in place. In addition, because housing is very expensive and even scarce in Silicon Valley, they were concerned that their children might be forced to leave the area as they grew older. Even if their children choose to relocate, the couple wanted a place for their adult children to be able to return to. They say that building an ADU felt like a happy obligation to them—a way to secure a future

Below: The siding and the roofing on the ADU are black corrugated metal in contrast with the wood cladding on the main house. Architect Adam Mayberry says, "The nondescript exterior of the ADU belies its tranquil and inviting interior, which serves as a peaceful retreat from the bustling city."

for their family, preserve their freedom to live in Silicon Valley, and possibly offer affordable housing options to others.

As the unit was completed, the owner's mother, who had previously shown little interest in living in the ADU, changed her mind due to the extensive repairs needed in her own home and her desire to be closer to her grandchildren. The ADU has met her needs perfectly.

DESIGNING THE ADU

Although David is a licensed architect, his expertise is primarily in the commercial realm and he does not specialize in the design of housing, particularly accessory dwelling units (ADUs). Therefore, when he needed a design for his own ADU, he consulted a housing industry friend who recommended Adam Mayberry, an architect who specializes in ADU design and had recently started his own firm.

GREEN FEATURES
- Heat recovery ventilator
- Induction cooktop
- Metal siding
- All electric (no gas coming into the house)

ENERGY FEATURES
- High efficiency insulation
- Mini-split heating/cooling
- Ceiling fans
- Electric heat pump water heater

Right: There are two lofts, one on each side of the unit, which provide both needed storage and short-term lodging. They have the added benefits of being conditioned space and providing natural light to the main living area. The couple say that although the lofts are suitable for sleeping, older occupants may be hesitant to utilize them due to physical limitations, while grandkids are likely to find them appealing.

Above: Multiple custom cabinets and appliance fronts fit seamlessly into the living room setting. The kitchen includes a small induction stove, cooktop, dishwasher, and refrigerator. (See sidebar on page 159.)

Opposite: Custom cabinetry fills an entire wall of the bedroom to provide adequate storage in the limited space of the room. With minimal wall space, the clerestory window brings in light without taking away needed wall space.

THE BARRYS' REQUIREMENTS

David had several must-have priorities, including addressing issues of noise and privacy, earthquakes, extreme heat, fire safety, accessibility, and sustainability. Energy efficiency, operating costs, thermal comfort, safety, and the impacts of the ADU on climate change were also major considerations. He wanted to maximize the available square footage and incorporate age-in-place features. During the design and permitting process, there were significant changes to the laws in California related to ADUs, and David says they took advantage of these changes to build a larger 900-square-foot, two-bedroom/two-bathroom unit, rather than the previously planned 750-square-foot, one-bedroom/one-bathroom unit. Despite the higher cost per square foot, they were willing to invest the extra time and money to redesign the unit and take advantage of the new regulations.

BUILDING WITH SIPS

David initially wanted to build the ADU with structural insulated panels (SIPs) because of their superior insulation, tighter sealing that reduces noise and air infiltration, and their greater resistance to thermal bridging and natural disasters. He was deterred from using SIPs because the local builders were not familiar with the material, and he subsequently chose to have the ADU stick built. However, with the rising cost of lumber during the pandemic, he and Adam decided to pursue building with SIPs despite the local attitudes of builders. Although SIPs may be generally more expensive than conventional construction methods, both architects decided that the higher quality, durability, faster building time, and high performance resulting in long-term energy and maintenance cost savings, made this method a good investment. They chose to keep the ADU all-electric, eliminating the health risks of gas leaks in this very tight building envelope.

AGE-IN-PLACE FEATURES

Gayle and David wanted the ADU to include age-in-place features. They included such items as wider doors (the front door is 42 inches wide and interior doors 36 inches), and levers instead of knobs on doors and faucets. Concrete flooring, except in the bathrooms, provides not only ease of movement but also the advantages of thermal mass. The walk-in shower is curbless, wheelchair accessible, and has two grab bars for safety. Sink counters are lower than average, so someone seated can access them. Outlets were raised to 18 inches from the floor rather than the typical 12 inches to make them more accessible. The closets are doorless and there are pocket doors for the bathrooms. Regular swing doors were used for both bedrooms, but all other interior spaces do not require doors.

SELECTING ENERGY AND SUSTAINABLE OPTIONS

The couple wanted the ADU to be durable and fire-resistant, particularly given the dry climate in northern California. Although the metal siding and roofing they chose was more expensive at the onset, it has a longer lifespan and needs less maintenance. The metal also pays tribute to the area's industrial heritage and creates a nice contrast with the historic wood clapboard siding on the main house, while also adding depth and texture to the facade. David says the metal siding and roofing were the perfect choice for the ADU, both practically and aesthetically.

With its energy-efficient design and the use of SIPs, the ADU hardly needed to be heated during the first winter in the unit, which was much colder and wetter than the average northern California winter.

Although there are some minor things David says he would have done differently, overall he says he is proud of what they have been able to accomplish with their ADU.

Above left: This barrier-free shower provides a clean, minimal appearance in this small space. The opaque window in the shower brings in light while also offering privacy.

Above right: The wall-hung toilet (see sidebar on page 167) uses minimal space and provides a clean, modern look.

Opposite: Several ceiling fans (see sidebar on page 185) in the living space help limit the need for air-conditioning and heating. The use of skylights and windows in the main living space and in each of the lofts creates a bright and airy atmosphere.

CEILING FANS

Ceiling fans don't actually cool the room, they move air, which carries heat away from the body, driving down body temperature in the warmer months. When no one is in the room, a spinning fan is just wasting electricity. Ceiling fans work counterclockwise in the warm months and should run in reverse in the colder months. This produces an updraft, forcing warm air near the ceiling down to where people are sitting. Ceiling fans lower energy usage and thus lower heating and cooling costs. ENERGY STAR-rated ceiling fans with light kits are 60 percent more efficient than conventional fan/light units and save on energy costs and protect the climate by reducing greenhouse gas emissions. They now come in many styles and sizes with a variety of speeds, blade pitch, and controls, and most come with remote controls.

MAZAMA MEADOW ADU

SITE-BUILT

LOCATION: Mazama, Washington

PHOTOGRAPHER
Stephen Brousseau
http://sbrousseauphoto.com

ARCHITECT
Dan Nelson
Designs Northwest Architects
www.designsnw.com

GENERAL CONTRACTOR
Impel Construction
https://impelconstruction.com

SIZE
1,020 square feet

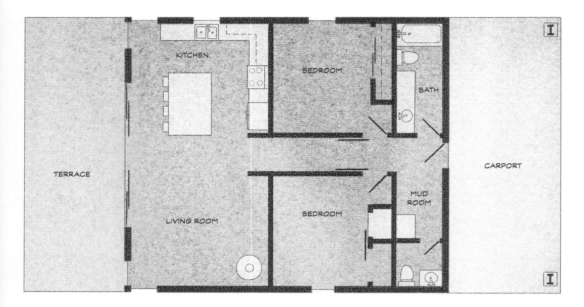

Colin and Alisa Sands built a vacation house in the North Cascades Mountains of Eastern Washington, a popular year-round outdoor recreation area with cross country skiing and snowmobiling in the winter and horseback riding, hiking, and river rafting in the summer. The couple later decided to live there permanently but found it lacked space for family and friends to visit and enjoy all the area had to offer. They decided to build the ADU so their guests could enjoy their visits there. The ADU was built with a full kitchen and lots of room so their guests could experience some independence while visiting.

The couple called on Dan Nelson and Matt Radach of Designs Northwest Architects, who built the main house. They wanted them to design this accessory unit using the same theme and concept as their primary home.

Below: The ADU sits to the side and front of the main house, affording both some privacy.

ENERGY EFFICIENCY

Colin and Alisa say energy efficiency is essential in this land they refer to as "the land of fire and ice." The hot summers can hit 108 degrees and extreme cold winters can sink to -30 F with five to eight feet of snow. In the winter the house is dependent on thermal mass from the concrete floors (see sidebar on page 193), a hydronic radiant floor system, and a wood-burning stove. Cooling strategies also depend on slab-on-grade construction, which acts as a thermal mass, and large fans for circulating air. These all help to regulate the temperature in the ADU without a forced-air system or air-conditioning. These strategies allow the home to stay quite comfortable without the use of air-conditioning even during the hottest weather which regularly exceeds 100 degrees.

GREEN FEATURES
- Metal roof with recycled content

ENERGY FEATURES
- Concrete floors
- Ceiling fans

Right: High ceilings and large windows and doors make the living room area expansive and bright, bringing in ample natural light and ventilation by catching the prevailing southerly breezes. Large glass doors connect the great room to a concrete terrace for outdoor entertaining. The concrete floors help to regulate the temperature through its thermal mass. The wood stove adds extra heat when needed in the cold winters.

FIRE PREVENTION AN ESSENTIAL PRIORITY

Because of the dry forested nature of this area, homes like this one are susceptible to wildfire. The Mazama Meadow house and ADU were designed to meet recommendations provided by the Firewise USA® Recognition Program, a national program administered by the National Fire Protection Association (NFPA) that encourages individuals to work together to reduce wildfire risk for their own homes, their neighbors' homes, and the entire community.

Special care was taken to incorporate a design to increase the wildfire resiliency of the Mazama Meadow ADU. Dan and Matt used several of these strategies including the use of fire-rated metal roofing, noncombustible steel support beams, slab-on-grade construction to prevent flames from moving through a crawl space, and open soffits. The landscape strategy incorporates rockeries and gabion walls as firebreaks. These were specifically designed to limit the use of combustible vegetation and large trees while utilizing a sprinkler system to keep the low-growing plants consistently well irrigated.

The ADU is designed to fit into the rustic nature of the area. The design utilizes a low-slope shed roof inspired by architecture seen in the region,

Opposite: The full kitchen provides guests the opportunity to cook for themselves when they desire. The large island seats four for a meal or for chatting with the cook.

Below: The front porch with the extended roofline provides a great place to relax in the shade.

which consists of mining, logging, and agricultural structures. Raw corrugated steel siding, weathered barn wood, and concrete floors are the primary materials used that further reinforce the local aesthetic. These low-maintenance materials were also selected in response to the environmental challenges of the region, which include extremes in temperature and the ongoing risk of fire.

According to Dan, "The environmental challenges of a site will often lead us to the appropriate design solution for the project. The form and the materials we incorporated into the Mazama Meadow ADU reflect the extreme environment in which we had to work."

Above: Large ceiling fans throughout the house circulate air and help keep the house comfortable in the warmer months.

CONCRETE FLOORS

Concrete flooring is becoming increasingly popular for both its aesthetics as well as its highly efficient way of helping to regulate the temperature inside the home. A concrete floor can soak up heat from direct sunlight during the day, store the heat, and release it slowly at night; this ability of concrete is called thermal mass.

A house can be designed to achieve a good deal of passive heating with concrete floors. Windows need to be designed and positioned in the home to allow as much of the sun's heat as possible to be absorbed by the floors. In summer, when the sun is higher in the sky, the floors should be mostly shielded from the sun with overhangs, so the house stays cool. Natural ventilation can also bring cool air into the house at night, allowing the flooring to absorb the cool air and release it during the day, as the air gets hotter.

In some cases, concrete is placed around the perimeter of the room close to windows to allow for the best exposure of the sun's heat; other materials can be used on the flooring in the center of the room. Concrete or other thermal mass materials (e.g., stone, masonry) can also be located close to a wood-burning stove, so the heat can be absorbed and released when the fire is out.

In the Mazama Meadow ADU the foundation also serves as the concrete floor, saving time, money, and resources. Heating and cooling a house this way improves air quality because, unlike a forced-air system, there's nothing blowing dust and pollutants through the air. Hydronic radiant floor heating systems are often used with concrete flooring and do double-duty in the summer when its piping is filled with chilled water.

Concrete floors require minimal maintenance, are long lasting, are relatively inexpensive, and can be designed with many different finishes and textures. The clean lines and easy maintenance of concrete floors has made them popular in new homes around the world.

THE LOFT ADU

SITE-BUILT

LOCATION: Monadnock Region, New Hampshire

PHOTOGRAPHER
Ryan Bent
www.ryanbent.com

ARCHITECT
Katie Sutherland
kcs Architects
https://kcs-architects.com

GENERAL CONTRACTOR
Niemela Construction LLC
Dublin, New Hampshire

SIZE
ADU 920 square feet
Garage 1,225 square feet

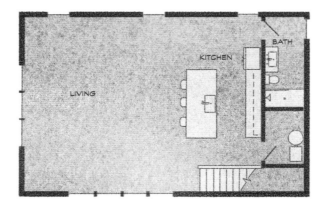

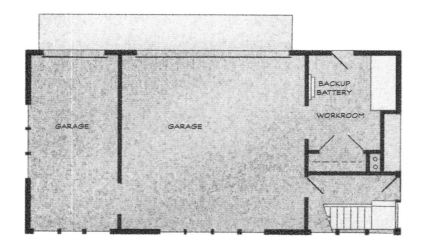

Owner Christine Clinton said rebuilding the garage was the final piece of a multi-decade project to renovate this historic property. She and her husband purchased this property in 1996 as a second home in an established community where they spent their summers with their children. In 2004, they moved to the house as their permanent residence and built on an extension—creating a more stripped-down neoclassical style that echoed features of the Federal style while creating a light-filled modern house for their growing family. In 2019 they decided to remodel the garage and add on an upper-level ADU.

The Loft ADU serves as a garage as well as a second-floor living/entertainment area.

AN ADDED SPACE

With growing children, Christine felt they needed more space. The new unit becomes a workout space when the college-age kids are home, hanging-out space with overnight accommodations for friends, a party space for the kids and adults, and an overflow guest space, "with the hope," says Christine, "that someday there will be grandchildren and extended family visits."

GREEN FEATURES
- Repurposed interior doors
- Quartz countertops
- Metal siding
- Marmoleum floors
- Alaskan yellow cedar pergola and interior stair wall

ENERGY FEATURES
- Solar panels
- LED lights
- Ceiling fans
- Backup battery source
- Hydronic radiant floor heating
- Solar hot water heat pump
- Car charger
- Insulated sheathing

Preceding overleaf: The Loft ADU serves as a garage as well as a second-floor living/entertainment area.

Right: The living area has several large windows adding an abundance of light and natural ventilation.

ENERGY EFFICIENCY

Christine says energy efficiency was very important to her since she was adding more square footage to an already large house. She knew that their direct southern exposure would enable them to create a situation where they could capture energy. Katie Sutherland of kcs Architects, the architect and designer for the ADU, also collaborated with Revision Energy on the rooftop solar system. The plan included a 10-kilowatt photovoltaic panel system on the roof, which satisfies all electricity and hot water needs for the house and ADU/garage space and then goes to the Tesla Powerwall system and ultimately supplies energy to the electrical grid. At night the house is largely powered by the battery Powerwall (see sidebar on page 202). The battery also works as a seamless backup system when the power is out, which happens frequently in this rural area with lots of trees. The loft/ADU has an electric hot water system which also serves the house's electric heat-pump. Christine says that over the past twelve months, their panels have supplied the grid with over 6,000 kilowatt-hours of power. Because the solar panels were producing so much excess energy, Christine bought a car charger for the new garage and then an electric car to start using some of this power.

Opposite left: Ceiling fans in the living area help to keep the house feeling cool in the hot summers. The pull-out couch in the living area provides a sleeping place for occasional guests.

Opposite right: The bathroom has a duel-flush, wall-hung toilet (see sidebar on page 167), which makes the room feel bigger. The shower has floor-to-ceiling subway tile, and the floors are the same Marmoleum as used throughout the unit.

Above: Two garages are on the lower level of the ADU—one for ping pong and sports gear, the other housing two cars.

WORKING ON A BUDGET

Christine says that cost was a constraint in the construction of the garage and ADU. She reduced the original size of the second-floor loft space to bring down the project cost, leaving a shed roof over the third garage bay. Marmoleum was used for all the flooring as an easy surface to maintain and a well-priced option. Kitchen components were stock items, also keeping the cost down. Christine says she splurged on the Alaskan yellow cedar wood accents on the stairs and pergola.

Although it was a challenge to complete construction during the pandemic with product delays and price increases for many of the materials, when the garage/ADU were completed Christine was delighted with the result. She says it was the final piece in the transformation of their property—making it work for her family while limiting or mitigating the energy usage and environmental impact of this large property. "We like to think we struck a good balance between preservation and modernization."

Opposite top: Two garages are on the lower level of the ADU—one for ping pong and sports gear, the other housing two cars.

Opposite bottom: The outside pergola provides a place to dine and relax outside.

Above: The brick section of the house was built in 1831 and was one of the original farms in the area. Christine gutted the Federal style brick portion of the house and relocated the front door to face Dublin Lake and Mount Monadnock. In 2004, the family moved to the house full-time and embarked on a renovation of the 1900s clapboard addition to the house, finishing the exterior with stucco for the south-facing facade and corrugated steel for the north. In 2019 Christine decided to replace the old garage with a new one and add an ADU.

BACKUP BATTERIES

Solar panels and backup batteries are a growing trend in this country, as people decide to limit their footprint on the planet by reducing their need for fossil fuel. Backup batteries store energy generated by the solar panels for use during extended periods of darkness, during cloudy weather, or when there are power outages. Most backup batteries today are lithium-ion batteries, which are more durable and efficient than other technologies. Backup batteries save money and provide security that the home will have energy in all situations.

Photovoltaics (PVs) use the sun to make electricity and feed that electricity to the main electrical panel for the property. When there is enough demand (consumption) on-site, the generated energy from the PV is used in "real time." When production exceeds on-site consumption, excess electrical production is stored in the battery. If the battery is full, surplus kilowatt-hours (kWhs) flow to the grid through a revenue grade meter. In New Hampshire, the current net-metering policy allows for monthly net metering, so this "surplus" kWhs can be used at times where consumption exceeds generation. During an outage, if there is no production, the house's critical loads panel draws kWhs from the Powerwall battery. If the array is generating kWhs during an outage, generation will continue to be used and stored on-site. The Powerwall has a storm watch feature that monitors the weather and stores electricity for potential power outages, which has been put to good use in the wilds of New Hampshire.

Backup batteries are sold by several companies. One of the most popular is the Tesla Powerwall which is on the Loft ADU. When choosing a backup battery, homeowners need to establish their household need and evaluate the battery's usable capacity (the amount of electricity stored in the battery that can be used—expressed in kilowatt-hours) and its power rating (the maximum amount of electricity a battery can discharge at one time, expressed in kilowatts.) Other considerations are cost and how many batteries will be needed; some can be configured with multiple units. Most companies offer a ten-year warranty on the batteries. On the Loft ADU, in addition to the backup battery, there is a car charger or electric vehicle supply equipment (EVSE). Battery backup systems are configured to collect a charge from the photovoltaic system. Therefore, even if a charger is configured to only take a charge from the electrical grid, with reverse metering it is effectively using power generated by the PVs, so the PV is indirectly charging the electric vehicle.

Below: The backup battery in the ADU provides energy to the ADU as well as the main house whenever the PVs are not delivering power on rainy days, at night, and when there is a power outage.

YUCCA ADU

SITE-BUILT

LOCATION: Yucca Valley, California

PHOTOGRAPHER
Eric Staudenmaier
www.ericstaudenmaier.com

ARCHITECT
ORA
www.ora.la

GENERAL CONTRACTOR
Joe Allen Construction

STRUCTURAL ENGINEER
Concorde Enterprises

SIZE
ADU 450 square feet total
Guest studio 254 square feet
Garage 248 square feet

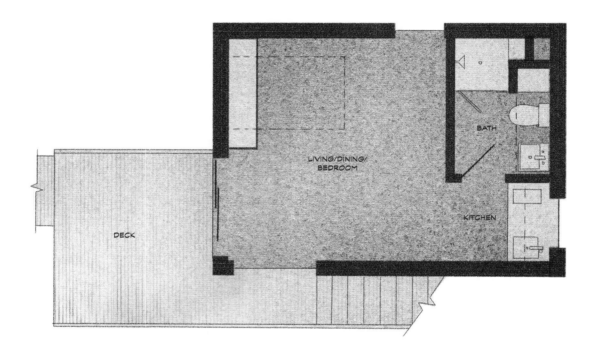

Opposite: Beneath the ADU is a garage that houses the washing machine, storage, and the couple's vintage teardrop camper.

Allison Morgan and Parke Skelton were looking for a place to escape their busy lives in Los Angeles and find a getaway for their family and friends. They purchased this secluded two and a half-acre parcel (which they later expanded to the original five-acre lot) adjacent to protected and undeveloped Bureau of Land Management (BLM) land just outside the town of Yucca Valley. When they bought the property there was an existing traditional but essentially abandoned gabled cabin nestled into the rocks, with several tiny outbuildings scattered across the property. The couple's

GREEN FEATURES

- Low flow toilet (0.9 gallons per flush)
- Low flow faucets and showerhead (1.5 gallons per minute)
- Linoleum flooring
- Sisal rug
- No VOC paint
- FSC certified plywood
- Ceramic tile seconds from a certified B Corporation and locally made to reduce carbon footprint

ENERGY FEATURES

- High performance windows and doors (with low-E glazing)
- High performance spray-in insulation to minimize air infiltration
- LED fixtures
- Cool roof
- ENERGY STAR appliances
- Tankless hot water heater
- Energy-efficient HVAC system
- Ceiling fan for passive cooling

original goal was to preserve and remodel the existing buildings as a weekend retreat for family and friends.

When the property was inspected, the local building agency condemned the existing buildings, most of which were built without permits. It would have been cost prohibitive to structurally upgrade them to meet current building codes, so the couple elected to start again with new structures.

BUILDING ANEW

Their new plan was to build energy efficient, economical, and sustainable structures that were respectful of the unique rocky surrounding environment. No existing rocks or trees were to be disturbed and new structures were to blend in with the land. Multiple buildings would allow the compound flexibility for large or small gatherings and evolve over time as the family's needs change.

Above: The ADU sits behind the main house, nestled in between large rock outcroppings.

Opposite top: The ADU opens to a porch, which expands the petite footprint of the unit.

Opposite bottom: Multiple windows and a sliding glass door provide natural ventilation as well as an abundance of light.

DEVELOPING A BUILDING PLAN

Despite the large parcel size, much of the land was unbuildable without disturbing the native rock formations. The couple called on architect Oonagh Ryan to come up with a plan to build two new independent structures in keeping with the scale of the original buildings on the site. An ADU was built along with the three-bedroom cabin. Multiple buildings were needed so that the compound could be flexible.

The ADU was designed to be an efficient addition to the main cabin. The compact, 254-square-foot studio space sits on top of a garage, providing flexible space for work, additional guests, or a quiet place of solitude. It bridges over the rock outcroppings, connecting directly to nearby hiking trails.

The 254-square-foot single car garage at the bottom level of the structure houses the washing machine, storage, and the owner's vintage teardrop camper, which can quickly be pulled out and used as an overflow bedroom when needed.

INTERIOR DESIGN

The interior of the suite was carefully planned to use every bit of space and to make it feel larger than it is. A Murphy bed (see sidebar on page 211) was installed to allow more floor space during the day when the bed was not being used. Green linoleum was rolled over the concrete surface to add warmth, and the furnishings were kept small scale and natural for this rustic environment. Natural materials and colors were used for the decor to reflect this very rustic environment. A small kitchen with a view and a set of mixed-color glazed tiles in the bathroom round out the space.

Overhangs around the periphery of the unit block out some of the hot sun, and ceiling fans and a mini-split system provide cool air when needed.

Although this ADU is quite small the owners say it has been a wonderful and useful addition to their vacation cabin.

Opposite top: Various seating areas were created in this small space.

Opposite bottom: The bathroom includes a vintage-style basin. The skylight brings natural light into the area.

Below: A small kitchen provides for essentials in the ADU.

Left: A comfortable sitting area feels expansive when the Murphy bed is closed.

Below: A Murphy bed (see sidebar on page 211) provides extra floor space when not in use. A fan and mini-split unit provide comfort in the hot weather.

MURPHY BEDS

When furnishing ADUs, it's an advantage to have multifunctional furniture or any furniture that saves space. Murphy beds or pull-down beds are a great option for areas where the bedroom or guestroom needs to double as a living room or office. They are mounted and vertically stored against the wall, or inside a cabinet, and are lowered for sleeping and concealed when not in use, creating extra floor space.

Wall beds are one type of Murphy bed, that is differentiated by the integration of the bed with cabinetry or shelves on the sides, below and/or above the bed. In a small space it is helpful to have the integrated shelving and cabinets for storage of extra blankets, pillows, bedding, clothing, and other essential items. Integrated LED lighting may also be part of the system. When these units are closed it can be difficult to recognize that the cabinetry includes a bed.

There are various lifting mechanisms available for Murphy beds, such as a piston or spring system or a manual opening mechanism. A spring-opening system is one of the earliest systems; the resistance of the spring is adjusted to make it easier to raise the bed and prevent its sudden retraction.

A piston-lifting system uses pressurized arms to lift and lower the bed. Manual systems have no pistons or springs, and they are opened and closed with just the user's manual strength.

In addition to providing extra floor space when not in use, these beds don't have to be remade every time they are used, unlike pullout beds. A built-in strap holds the bedding in place when not in use. Like other beds, they can also be moved if there is a change of residence.

Murphy beds do not generally have box springs. The mattress is attached to the bed frame with a retention system, like an elastic strap, that holds the mattress to the bed frame. Standard mattresses can be used but must adhere to the maximum thickness suggested by the manufacturer—usually eight to twelve inches.

Murphy beds are available from many online and big box retailers as well as specialty retailers. These beds have recently become increasingly popular with the rise in ADUs, small apartments, and small houses. The Murphy bed in the Yucca ADU was custom built.

ST. ANDREWS ADU

SITE-BUILT

LOCATION: Hancock Park, California

PHOTOGRAPHER
Yoshihiro Makino
www.yoshimakino.us

ARCHITECT
Assembledge+
www.assembledge.com

GENERAL CONTRACTOR
Brunswick Builders

LANDSCAPE DESIGN
Outer Space Landscaping
www.bestlagardens.com

SIZE
708 square feet

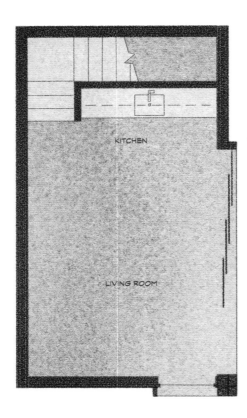

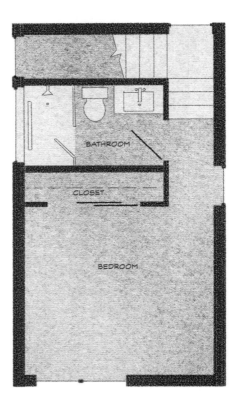

Opposite: Fiber cement siding on the ADU matches the color of the existing 1919 Craftsman bungalow that was already there. Large windows provide abundant light in this small structure.

As their kids got older, Joanna and Steve Vernetti realized they needed more space. They loved their house and wanted to stay in it, but it was feeling too small. So they decided to build an ADU and an extension to the main house, which they say was "an ideal solution" to their space issue. Currently their teenage son, Bruno, (one of their three children) is using the second-floor bedroom and bathroom, and the living space downstairs is shared by the whole family. In the future they will use the ADU for guests.

GREEN FEATURES
- Fiber cement siding
- Xeriscape landscaping

ENERGY FEATURES
- Cement flooring
- LED lighting
- Mini-split heating/cooling

DESIGN OF THE ADU

The couple wanted a modern aesthetic for the ADU, but one that would meld with the Craftsman-style bungalow originally built in 1916. The homeowners reached out to David Thompson, the principal and founder of Assembledge+, a long-time friend of the couple who had designed their restaurant, Vernetti, in Larchmont Village, Los Angeles.

Thompson says, "This project is an excellent example of the many opportunities for properties throughout Los Angeles. Thanks to the moderate California climate, we can extend the living spaces outdoors, reactivate these rear-yard spaces, and transport a negative space like a garage into an activated area for people to gather."

Together the couple chose a very sustainable and low-maintenance fiber cement siding in a color that would complement their original house. They chose concrete for the lower level of the ADU to serve as thermal mass and for its beautiful aesthetics. The concrete floor is durable, and it allows the exterior finishes to feel like they are flowing into the space, blurring the lines between indoor and outdoor.

Energy efficiency was important to them but was also a requirement to meet the strict energy requirements of the City of Los Angeles. Large windows and doors bring in lots of natural light and ventilation.

Opposite: The sliding glass door expands the feeling of space in the living area along with bringing in a good deal of light and fresh air.

Below: The first-floor kitchenette includes an under-counter refrigerator. There is no cooktop, although the design does allow for venting, so it could easily be installed later. Concrete floors add a modern touch to this space while also providing thermal mass, releasing warmth in the evening on cooler days.

CREATING MORE OUTDOOR SPACE

The main design challenge, the couple says, was creating a harmonious connection between the new ADU with the existing house—making sure that the connections were unobstructed and naturally flowing. However, by building the addition and the ADU, it created a courtyard that is more functional than it was previously.

Although there were challenges extending a 100-year-old house and making it work aesthetically with modern construction, they are so happy with the result they have forgotten the trials and tribulations of building. Joanna says they consider the space between the house and the ADU as an outdoor room that bridges the gap between the two buildings. They used both concrete and wood on the exterior surfaces to break up and define the space.

The couple says, "We love the additional space and the proximity of the ADU and house which now makes our backyard and outdoor space feel like another living area. We have not only gained indoor space, but very usable outdoor space as well."

Right: A courtyard is created with the juxtaposition of the main house and the newly created ADU. The patio was newly constructed when the addition and ADU were built, unifying the properties.

Above: The tiled barrier-free shower with a frameless shower door gives the room a spacious feel while also providing a safe showering experience. The window high on the wall brings in light while maintaining privacy.

BARRIER-FREE SHOWERS

Barrier-free, or curbless, walk-in showers that are designed to provide a safe and convenient shower experience are growing in popularity. A curbless shower floor is flush with the rest of the bathroom flooring and safe for people with disabilities as well as healthy adults. It eliminates the risk of tripping on a curb getting into a shower, and adheres to the concept of Universal Design, which specifies that design should be accessible to all people at every stage of their changing lives.

Barrier-free showers must be constructed with the slope of the floor directing the water toward the drain, keeping the water in the shower area. Some barrier-free showers are created with prefabricated shower trays, which are flush with the rest of the bathroom floor. Other barrier showers are custom made with a sloped mortar bed. Wet rooms are also becoming more common. These are showers with no barriers that share the bathroom space without separating walls. In this situation, the flooring needs to be sloped toward the floor drain as well.

SUPPLIERS

ZUMETTE ADU

CertainTeed (insulation, roofing, water resistant barrier, interior moisture and air retarder, and drywall)
www.certainteed.com

Electrolux (stacked washer and dryer)
www.electrolux.com

Fisher & Paykel (induction range, microwave hood, microwave, dishwasher, French door refrigerator)
www.fisherpaykel.com

James Hardie (siding)
www.jameshardie.com

Kahrs (flooring)
www.kahrs.com

Lifebreath (heat recovery ventilator)
www.lifebreath.com/us/

Kohltech (tilt-turn windows)
www.kohltech.com

Masonite (main entry door)
https://residential.masonite.com

Mitsubishi Electric (heat pump)
www.mitsubishicomfort.com/residential

SONOMA VALLEY A-FRAME

Anderson Windows
www.andersonwindows.com

Breville (microwave)
www.breville.com/us/

Fulgor Milano (stove)
www.fulgor-milano.com/us/en/

Herman Miller (upstairs bedroom pendant)
https://store.hermanmiller.com

IKEA (cabinets)
www.ikea.com

James Hardie (fiber cement siding)
www.jameshardie.com

La Cantina (large glass sliding-door)
www.lacantinadoors.com

LZF (dining room pendant)
https://lzf-lamps.com

Nest (smart thermostat)
https://nest.com/thermostats

Mitsubishi (ducted mini-split system)
www.mitsubishicomfort.com

Moooi (spiral stair pendant)
www.moooi.com/us/

Porcelanosa (tile floors and walls)
www.porcelanosa-usa.com

Salter Spiral Stair (spiral staircase)
www.salterspiralstair.com

Smeg (refrigerator and dishwasher)
www.smeg.com/us

Velux (skylights)
www.veluxusa.com

Water's Edge Woods (oak paneling)
www.watersedgewoods.com

Zephyr (range hood)
https://zephyronline.com

ARGYLE ADU

Architessa (tile)
https://architessa.com

Caesarstone (quartz countertops)
www.caesarstoneus.com

Chiltrix (heat pump, hot water tank)
www.chiltrix.com

Corian (bathroom countertops)
www.corian.com

KitchenAid (convection oven, microwave, exhaust hood)
www.kitchenaid.com

LG (washer/dryer)
http:///lg.com/us/laundry

Miele (induction cooktop, dishwasher)
www.mieleusa.com

Modern Fan Co. (ceiling fans)
https://modernfan.com/ceiling-fans

Mosa (tile)
www.mosa.com/en-us

Panasonic (energy recovery ventilator)
http://na.panasonic.com

Pella (windows and doors)
www.pella.com

Thermador (refrigerator/freezer)
www.thermador.com/us

TruExterior (siding and trim)
https://truexterior.com

CANTERBURY ADU

Caesarstone (countertops)
www.caesarstoneus.com

Cedar and Moss (kitchen pendants)
https://cedarandmoss.com

Clay Imports (bathroom tiles)
https://clayimports.com

Elisa Pisano Tile (cement tiles)
www.elisapassino.com/cement-tiles

Kitchen Aide (appliances)
www.kitchenaide.com

Minka Aire (ceiling fan)
www.minkagroup.net/minka-aire

CLAYTON STREET ADU

Mitsubishi (mini-split HVAC)
www.mitsubishicomfort.com

Velux (skylights)
www.veluxusa.com

FERN STREET ADU

Daikin (ducted mini-split system)
https://daikincomfort.com

Hunter (ceiling fan)
www.hunterfan.com

James Hardie (fiber cement siding)
www.jameshardie.com

Lummus Supply Co. (double-hung windows)
www.lummussupply.com

Sherwin Williams (paint)

PLYMOUTH ADU

Ann Sacks (ceramic tile)
www.annsacks.com

CertainTeed (roofing)
www.certainteed.com

Fujitsu (mini-split system)
www.fujitsu-general.com/us

James Hardie (fiber cement siding)
www.jameshardie.com

Western Window Systems (bifold doors, windows, and doors)
https://westernwindowsystems.com

SUNFLOWER ADU

Arbor Wood (exterior wood siding)
https://arborwoodco.com

Broan (energy recovery ventilator)
www.broan-nutone.com

Curava (recycled glass surfaces)
www.curava.com

EPS Buildings (SIPs)
www.epsbuildings.com

IKEA (kitchen cabinets, sinks, and faucets)
www.ikea.com

LP Building Solutions (engineered wood siding)
https://lpcorp.com

Marvin Windows
www.marvin.com

Mitsubishi (mini-splits)
www.mitsubishicomfort.com

Velux (skylights)
www.veluxusa.com
www.sherwin-williams.com

PARKWAY LANEWAY

Centra Windows
https://www.centrawindows.com/

Daltile (tile)
www.daltile.com

Ikea (cabinetry)
https://www.ikea.com/ca/en/

James Hardie (fiber cement siding)
www.jameshardie.ca

Kuzco Lighting
www.Kuzcolighting.com

Mitsubishi (heat pump and HRV)
www.mitsubishicomfort.com

Nudura (insulating concrete forms)
www.nudura.com

Riobel (plumbing fixtures)
http://robel.design/en

West Eco Panels (structural insulated panels)
www.WestEcoPanels.com

BEECH HAUS ADU

Basco Appliances (washer, dryer, small water heater, small refrigerator)
www.bascoappliances.com

James Hardie (fiber cement siding)
www.jameshardie.com

Mitsubishi (mini-split system)
https://discover.
mitsubishicomfort.com

Ply Gem (windows and sliding
door)
www.plygem.com

SOUTH SOUND ADU

James Hardie (siding)
www.jameshardie.com

Kohler (toilet)
www.kohler.com/en

Milgard (windows and doors)
www.milgard.com

Mitsubishi Electric (mini-split
system)
https://discover.
mitsubishicomfort.com

3-Day Blinds (Honeycomb
twin-cell blinds)
www.3dayblinds.com

COMER ADU

Bosch (wall oven and
dishwasher)
www.bosch-home.com

Simpson (exterior doors)
www.simpsondoor.com

Jeldwen (interior doors)
www.jeld-wen.com

Kohler (wall-hung toilet,
actuator plate, shower)
www.kohler.com/en

Miele (washer, heat pump
dryer)
www.mieleusa.com

Sharp (microwave drawer)
www.sharpusa.com

Simpson (interior doors)
www.simpsondoor.com

Subzero (refrigerator)
www.subzero-wolf.com

ThermaTru (garage door)
www.thermatru.com

Wolf (cooktop)
www.subzero-wolf.com

GREEN HOUSE ADU

BamDeck (decking)
www.calibamboo.com

Broan (heat recovery
ventilator)
www.broan-nutone.com

Caesarstone (quartz
countertops)
www.caesarstoneus.com

Ecobee (smart thermostat)
www.ecobee.com

Fisher & Paykel (undercounter
refrigerator)
www.fisherpaykel.com/us

GE Profile (induction stove)
www.geappliances.com

Heliene (solar panels)
https://heliene.com

IKEA (kitchen cabinets)
www.ikea.com/us/

Marmoleum (linseed oil-based
linoleum flooring)
www.forbo.com

Milestone Tiles (high friction
tile)
www.milestonetiles.com

NTI (on-demand hot water
heater)
https://ntiboilers.com

Trespa (exterior wood panels)
www.trespa.com/en

Warmboard (radiant heating)
www.warmboard.com

ART COLLECTORS' ADU

Daltile (bathroom tiles)
www.daltile.com

Duravit (wall-hung toilet)
www.duravit.us

Franke (kitchen faucets)
www.franke.com

Grohe (bathroom fixtures)
www.grohe.us

Mendota (gas fireplace)
https://mendotahearth.com

Subzero (refrigerator)
www.subzero-wolf.com

Takagi (tankless water heater)
www.takagi.com

Wolf (cooktop and wall oven)
www.subzero-wolf.com

HAMILTON COURT ADU

Amba Quadro (heated towel
rack)
https://ambaproducts.com

Body Glove (water filtration)
https://bodyglove.waterinc.
com

Bosch (microwave with
convection, induction cooktop
and oven)
www.bosch-home.com

Dankin (mini-split system)
https://daikincomfort.com

Fisher & Paykel (French door
refrigerator, double drawer
dishwasher)
www.fisherpaykel.com

Grohe (bathroom fixtures)
www.grohe.us

James Hardie (fiber cement
siding and trim)
www.jameshardie.com

Kohler (sinks and medicine
cabinet)
www.kohler.com

Miele (washing machine,
smart heat pump dryer, and
stacking kit)
www.mieleusa.com

Nuheat (electric radiant floor heating)
www.nuheat.com

Rinnai (tankless water heater)
www.rinnai.us

Seachrome (grab bars)
https://seachrome.com

Simonton (windows)
www.simonton.com

Simpson Door Company (entry and French doors)
www.simpsondoor.com

Toto (toilet)
www.totousa.com

Zephyr (exhaust hood)
https://zephyronline.com

LANGFORD AVENUE LANEWAY

American Olean (ceramic tile)
www.americanolean.com

Benjamin Moore (paint)
www.benjaminmoore.com

Bosch (dishwasher)
www.bosch-home.com/us

Caesarstone (countertops)
www.caesarstoneus.com

Richelieu (hardware)
www.richelieu.com/us/en

Stone Tile (engineered flooring)
https://stone-tile.com

Toto (hanging toilet)
www.totousa.com

CEDAR COTTAGE ADU

Anderson (exterior windows and doors)
www.renewalbyandersen.com

Beko (24-inch refrigerator)
www.beko.com

Fisher & Paykel (dish-drawer dishwasher)
www.fisherpaykel.com/us

Grohe (bathroom fixtures)
www.grohe.us

Mitsubishi (mini-split heat pump)
https://discover.mitsubishicomfort.com

MARION AVENUE ADU

Franke (kitchen sink)
www.franke.com/us/en

GE (oven)
www.geappliances.com

Geeni (front door light switch)
https://mygeeni.com

Grohe (shower fixtures)
www.grohe.us

Hansgrohe (kitchen faucet)
www.hansgrohe-usa.com

Hauschen (LED lighted mirror)
www.hauschenhome.com

Horow (toilet)
https://horowbath.com

Kenyan (induction cooktop)
www.cookwithkenyon.com

LG (under-counter smart washer/dryer, refrigerator)
www.lg.com

Mitsubishi (mini-split system)
www.mitsubishicomfort.com

SILVER LAKE ADU

Atlantis Rail Systems (exterior railing)
www.atlantisrail.com

Franke (fixtures)
www.franke.com/us

Kohler (wall-hung toilet)
www.kohler.com

Subzero (refrigerator/freezer)
www.subzero-wolf.com

Wolf (induction stove)
www.subzero-wolf.com

ADA PLUS

Astria Fireplaces
https://astria.us.com

Caesarstone (quartz countertops)
www.caesarstoneus.com

Miele (wall oven, cooktop)
www.mieleusa.com

Mitsubishi (mini-split systems)
www.mitsubishicomfort.com

Sub Zero (under-counter refrigerator)
www.subzero-wolf.com

SEVENS ADU

Anderson (windows and doors)
www.andersenwindows.com

Big Ass Fans
https://bigassfans.com

Bosch (induction cooktop, oven)
www.bosch-home.com

California Closets
www.californiaclosets.com

Fakro (skylights)
www.fakrousa.com

Fisher & Paykel (refrigerator)
www.fisherpaykel.com

Lunos (heat recovery ventilator)
https://lunoscanada.com

Miele (washer and dryer)
www.mieleusa.com

Rheem (electric heat pump water heater)
www.rheem.com

Samsung (mini-split system)
www.samsung.com

Thermador (dishwasher)
www.thermador.com/us

MAZAMA MEADOW ADU

Anderson (windows)
www.andersenwindows.com

ARC Surfaces (quartz countertops)
https://arcsurfaces.com

Barnlight (lighting)
www.barnlight.com

Canyon Creek (cabinets)
www.canyoncreek.com

Danfoss heat cables (radiant floor heat)
www.danfoss.com

FLOR (area rugs)
www.flor.com

LG Black Stainless Steel (appliances)
www.lg.com/us/

Minka Aire (ceiling fans)
www.minkagroup.net

Morso (pedestal wood stove)
https://morsoe.com/us

THE LOFT ADU

Big Ass Fans
https://bigassfans.com

Creations in Stone (quartz)
http://creationsinstoneofkeene.com

dweLED (LED lights)
www.build.com

IKEA (kitchen cabinets and bath vanity)
www.ikea.com

Marmoleum (flooring)
www.forbo.com

Marvin Doors and Windows
www.marvin.com

Revision Energy (photovoltaic system)
www.revisionenergy.com

Tesla Powerwall (battery)
www.tesla.com/powerwall

YUCCA ADU

Abet Laminati (kitchen countertop and shelves: Baltic birch plywood, plastic laminate)
https://abetlaminati.com/en/

Alape (bathroom bucket sink)
https://www.alape.com

Delta (bath faucet and showerhead)
https://www.deltafaucet.com

Elkay (kitchen sink)
www.elkay.com/us/en.html

Eurodib (cooktop)
https://eurodib.com/

Forbo (laminate)
https://www.forbo.com

General Electric (refrigerator)
www.frigidaire.com

Heath Ceramics (tile)
https://www.heathceramics.com/

LG (washer and dryer)
https://www.lg.com/us

Mitsubishi (mini-split system)
www.mitsubishicomfort.com

Toto (toilet)
https://www.totousa.com

SAINT ANDREWS ADU

Carrier (mini-split system)
www.carrier.com

Fleetwood (windows and doors)
www.fleetwoodusa.com

CertainTeed (roof shingles)
www.certainteed.com

James Hardie (fiber cement siding)
www.jameshardie.com